Cruisin' Thru Life
Dip Street
and
Other Miracles

The Miracle of...

Cruisin' Thru Life
Dip Street
and
Other Miracles

By Peggy Purser Freeman

Dedication

***To the small-town communities that gave us a
quality of life like none other, a special thank you
and prayers for a future as blessed as the past.***

To Dickey Freeman, my husband, who has loved,
protected and provided for me for fifty years: You not only
help me remember the past, you are the promise of my
tomorrows. And today you help me remember where I put
my keys, glasses, purse...

**To my daughters, Stephanie Nance and Cynthia
Freeman-Wilson**: You are my best friends and your
encouragement enables me to create.

**To my grandson, Tanner Beaty Freeman-DeJohn
Wilson and my beautiful granddaughters, Makayla
Nance and Alicia Wilson,** All three of you are better
writers than I will ever be. You are my heart.

The Miracle of...

Special Acknowledgment

To those who were with me on Dip Street many times and those who have helped with this project: Patsy Lewis Hooten, Ann Wallace Hooks, Nita Stockett, Sheran Morris Childress, Lillie Hutson Morris, Donna Jennings Bolton, Lana Payne Barnett and Jan Doan Meador, thank you. All the members of "Remember in Tulia Facebook Group," including Johnny Barnhart, Oran Watson and others who stir my memories and infuse my today with fellowship, bless you.

An extra measure of appreciation goes to my sister-in-law, Micah Diane Purser, for her skills in proofing. Brandon Sims, (who is like his mom, my sister Ruth) has encouraged me all year, set up web pages and even cleaned my computer.

A special thanks to the Granbury Writers' Bloc for their help, encouragement and friendship, and also to Connie Leonard, who even prayed I would finish this book on deadline. Each member of the critique groups I've been in over the years, has given me part of their most valuable possession—they've given their time.

Thank you, North Texas Romance Writers Association (NTRWA) and Cleburne Writers and North Texas Society of Children's Book Writers and Illustrators (NTSCBWI). Critique partners like Lori Wilde, Margo Carmichael, Gwen LaVert, Emily Howse, and Christine Crocker and wonderful book friends like Alan Stacy and Diane Roberts, "You complete me"... and check my spelling. I love you all.

Special recognition goes to Johnny Young for the wonderful black and white photo of Dip Street.

Table of Contents

Driving Down Dip With Your Kids

Senior Citizens Dragging Dip Street

A History of Dip Street

by Lana Payne Barnett

If bricks could talk, the ones on West Broadway in Tulia, Texas would say PLENTY. Also known as Dip Street, this stately avenue became the "drag." For generations, teenagers made the street their personal territory.

The bricks were laid in the early 1920s, not long after the first automobiles arrived in Tulia. Not long after, kids made the brick road their "drag." So…if your grandparents grew up in Tulia, you can be sure, they could be found on the iconic street. It may have been your ancestors who created the rules to maneuver the dips located at each intersection. These Dip Street rules can also apply to life.

While cruising, one "necessity" was to creep along at about five miles an hour so you didn't knock the bottom out of your parent's car. Another purpose for driving at that speed; it allowed you to 'see and be seen.'

Another rule that made you a Dip Street "professional" was to take the dips at an angle, different angles for different dips. If you saw someone hit a dip straight-on, you knew they were a novice.

Teens made the trek, thousands of times, to the old Santa Fe Depot, made a U-turn, back up Dip to the Ozark Trail Monument, another U-turn and back again. Oh, and you honked at everyone, even if you had just honked five minutes before.

If bricks could talk they may tell of the teens in the 1940s, according to Marge Dawson, that would see how fast they could drive between the two telephone poles that sat about fifteen feet apart in front of the Depot. They may tell you of the many shade trees that once graced the center of the street and how, after they were removed, Tulia teens would park in that center to talk and laugh and make memories.

Tulia's youth were not the only ones to make use of the grand, old ten-block stretch. Teens from other towns, throughout the Panhandle and South Plains region knew it was a great place to hang out.

And ... if they could talk, the bricks could tell you that I introduced a couple in front of Wallace Funeral Home who later became man & wife; that Olive Love met the love of her life, Ted Bradley, on Dip; and that Ricky Cox met his wife there. Best of all was the night I met my husband. I was riding around with a friend when he pulled us over and asked us to get in their car and ride with him and his friend. We accepted.

These are just a few of my stories; the bricks could tell you so many more. They could tell you that, sadly, kids today no longer cruise Dip. I don't know where they hang out, but they have abandoned the old street.

I would like to say thank you to Peggy Purser Freeman for relating memories of a bygone era, and more. It will be something we can read and recall and cherish as a piece of our childhood. She will always be the little sister to my sweet and dear friend, Ouida. When we were teenagers, Ouida frequently stayed at my house; often the first place we headed was to Dip Street. I remember one time in particular a little sister was with us. So...what do you do with little sisters when you are supposed to be so "cool?" You make them lie down in the back seat and hide, of course.

Lana Payne Barnett is an author, columnist, publisher and past Tulia Chamber of Commerce president. Her books include: *Lonely Graves, a Texas Murder Trilogy* and *Presenting the Texas Panhandle.* Other published works include: "Woman's Ink," "Who's Who-Women of the Panhandle," and "Route 66-Guide to the Texas Panhandle," and "Redneck Reunion" a two-act comedy. Her Facebook page [Facebook.com/pages/Panhandle-Tidbits] with over 10,500 readers. She and her husband live in Tulia, Texas.

Dip Street Update

Since the first printing of this book, Lana and I have instigated a Dip Street Fest on the Friday night before Picnic in Tulia (usually the weekend closest to July 17th). Lana received permission from the police department and city officials. Then many of our friends on Facebook helped to spread the word. The first event in 2014 exceeded our expectations with over 200 cars, trucks and even huge trailers, carrying an entire class, all cruised Dip Street like they did in the good old days. Now Dip Fest is planned each year during the Picnic weekend.

Introduction ... Draggin' Dip Street

Memories of my hometown and Dip Street are to me, summer rain to the dry, thirsty soil.

Like most miracles, "the drag" is a time machine that transports us back to a season of firsts—first drive, first kiss, first break-up, first traffic-ticket and more. Our memories wrap around the familiar drag like the cars once did, cruising around with oldies-but-goodies blaring from the radio and laughter cajoling us to happier days.

Dip Street in my hometown warms me with those memories of growing up in the best of times. With each twist and turn (and dip) we learned, loved and discovered who we were. The drag stands today as an icon of an era when we believed in miracles.

For those "Baby Boomers" blessed enough to be a teenager back in the day when gas sold for thirty-cents a gallon, the local drag represents the world's greatest ride.

In that time "the car" supposedly defined who you were. But the miracles of those good years included more than cheap gas. We believed in racial equality, tearing down an iron curtain and walking on the moon. The miracles came true, one dream at a time. Miracles to me aren't big, unbelievable events that rarely happen. Miracles are small events that happen every day. If you aren't careful you will miss them.

This book isn't just about cruising the main drag. It's about life and learning to take the dips, the curves and the potholes. The slice-of-life stories included in this book were written over the years. Some, I wrote for the Swisher County News. Others were previously published in *Chicken Soup for the Soul* books. The rest seem to pour out of my heart with the need to share. I hope these stories will cause the winds of yesterday to blow across your mind and strengthen your faith.

THE MIRACLE of...

Draggin' Dip In the Backseat

Being the Baby

My life began in a dresser drawer because there was no room for a baby crib in our two room house in South Dallas. The small house bulged with the noise and activities of my four brothers, three sisters and mom and dad. I grew up in various small towns in the Panhandle of Texas as my family moved from one broken-down farmhouse to another, working as sharecroppers.

In my family, work was expected, however, being the youngest, I found time to daydream. I only received two spankings from my father in my life. It only took two. Actually one worked, but I didn't think before I spoke.

The first spanking was punishment for using the GD curse word when I was about five. My cat ripped my finger with his little sharp claws and I shouted out the curse. Daddy walked calmly to mom's closet and pulled out a thin leather belt covered in tiny bumps. It would have been a 911 call in today's world. Confused, I cried, "But you say it all the time." That was the last time I accidentally said a curse word.

The other spanking involved a Cotton-T. I may have been six or seven that fall. We were working a dry-land farm near Ralls or Lorenzo. My two brothers could each pull a hundred pounds of cotton a day. Daddy raced Nolan for top honors each day. Mom was tireless in her work, pulling cotton all day, preparing a meal, and washing and cleaning at night. Ruth, who would have been thirteen or fourteen at the time, had most of the cooking and some ironing done before we reached the house. Ouida never stopped. No one was sure what she was doing, but she never stopped.

After lunch I quickly pulled enough cotton to make a nice soft pillow in the end of my sack. Then I spread it under a row of cotton stalks that gave the semblance of a shade tree. I stretched out and shut my eyes, only to be awakened by my dad's calm, but stern, voice.

"Peggy, what are you doing?" he asked.

"I'm taking a nap." I used my cute voice, the one every baby of the family develops to use at times like those.

"Why aren't you working like the rest of the family?" My dad used the stern voice that dads develop to use at times like this.

I looked up and smiled. "Because I'm the baby and I don't have to work."

Life Lessons: If you're a kid, don't ever sass your dad in the middle of a cotton-field where the closest switch is a cotton stalk. That day I learned the meaning of the term "Cotton T."

Eagles Pipping

Eagles are amazing! Each year I watch the live eagle camera set up in Iowa and wonder if any eagles have nested near my house. The eagle provides us with so many parables. Currently I'm editing a book I've written over the years about the attributes and habits of the majestic bird.

When eagles hatch, it's a time-consuming, difficult task. If you have ever watched the process of a bird or chicken hatching, you know the intense desire to help the frail life in its struggle to get out of the egg. But if you've been raised by a wise mother or dad, you know not to help. With my mom, it was part of the "Don't Meddle, Don't Touch" song and wisdom. She often sang the song and then gave a tidbit of knowledge about nature.

The egg is like a workout room for the little eaglet—a gymnasium to build its muscles and provide the strength it needs to survive. If interrupted or hurried, the bird dies. I heard that it's an extremely sad sight to watch the baby bird try to survive when hatching is interrupted. Eaglets break through the shell by using their egg tooth, a pointed bump on the top of the beak. It sometimes takes from twelve to forty-eight hours to hatch after making the first break in the shell. This is called pipping.

The eagles at Decorah, on the banks of the babbling waters of Trout Run in extreme northeast Iowa, nest in a cottonwood tree on private property near the Decorah Fish Hatchery (operated by the Iowa Department of Natural Resources). It's all about LOCATION, LOCATION,

LOCATION. What better place to build a nest for hungry babies than near a fish factory?

Location is important. This is why a small town is such a great place to raise kids. Time is a rare commodity. In the country, time slows to an armadillo crawl. There's another attribute in the lives of those who settled our country— tenacity like that of the eagle. Time and tenacity will carry us through tough situations.

Tenacity is a trait that is difficult to allow your children to develop. You want them to stop what they are doing in order to move on to what you need them to do next. Our "hurry, hurry lifestyle" fosters the opposite of tenacity. No one has time to stick to a project.

Most things in life have been easy for me. However, I have worked for twenty years to learn to play a mountain dulcimer. Yes, I took piano as a girl and I'm sure my teacher suffered greatly. She was only a teenager, yet very patient and sweet. The notes and lines all merged together just as letters and words did for me. I remember a bit from the few months I took lessons. The same problem occurred while trying to play tabs on the dulcimer.

On the dulcimer a fret is called a number and therefore you play by numbers. My brain is totally allergic to numbers. After fifteen years of trying to play, I finally picked up the dulcimer, put away the music and went outside. I let my fingers slide up and down the frets until I found the tune I sang. Tenacity has finally birthed music--not excellent, but at least people can tell what I'm playing.

Life Lessons: Time for tenacity is one of the greatest gifts you can give your children. When we're in a hurry, we finally finish the task for the child. When we help a child too much, they don't learn to finish; they learn to let someone else do it for them. They often think their efforts didn't please us and this develops into low self-esteem. Make time for teaching tenacity. Puzzles help foster that stick-to-it-until-it's-done mentality and games of all kinds help build character. Children develop best when given the time to grow--the time of pipping.

The Tallest Girl

I remember weighing 35 pounds. And I was the tallest girl in the third grade. And worse than that, at mid-term the teacher told me I wouldn't be going to fourth grade because I couldn't read. Either I did better in reading, or I would have to repeat the grade.

I looked at all the squiggly lines on the pages of *Tip and Mitten*. Reading was too hard. Besides I could make up better stories in my imagination than a dog hiding in the leaves. "Here, Tip. Where's Tip?" But I did want to go to fourth grade. I could just see me eight-feet-tall and still in third grade. So I read.

I read to everyone who would listen, even Sally the cow. I worked and I worked. Then one day it happened. I loved reading. I made it to fourth grade with my class. That December we moved to Tulia where fifth grade was housed in the junior-high building. I loved school, thanks to teachers like Mrs. Massey. About this time I discovered the library. I read every Nancy Drew book the librarian had in the Swisher County Library.

I still couldn't spell and usually made an "F" on my English papers. I didn't care about grammar. I thought since I couldn't spell, it didn't matter. I wrote really messy, hoping the teacher wouldn't know if it was an "E" or an "I." It didn't work. The teacher thought I was dumb and messy.

Then in high school, I had a wonderful teacher who gave two grades—one for the story I wrote and the other grade for how it made her feel and how my words fit together. I made my first "A." Of course there was an "F" below it, but I made my first excellent grade on a writing paper. That "A" made me think I had something good inside me, something I could share with others.

Years later that the desktop computer came along, and now I'm an author. I especially love writing for children. I never dreamed I'd be able to write, but my teacher thought I could. My mom thought I could. My sisters thought I could. Therefore, I write.

I believe we can do most anything, if we keep trying. Each day is like a panhandle horizon waiting for our unique, God-given abilities to rise and shine on the world.

Life Lessons: Tell stories and read to your children. Start before they're born. Stop when they're 99. Family storytelling and reading develops vocabulary and bonds you together. It promotes values and builds faith. We need those two things desperately in today's world.

The Big Family Football Game

Texans cut their baby teeth on football. As the youngest of eight, I spent my formative years watching my brothers play. My sister, Ladell, twirled and marched at Crozier Tech in Dallas. I sat in "the grandstands beating on a tin can, saying, 'Who can? We can! Nobody else can. What? Win this game!'"(as the very old cheer goes). I screamed as my brothers David and Nolan ran up and down grassy fields, from Wills Point to Idalou, from Ralls to Lorenzo. I worshiped my hero, Nolan, as he played for Texas Tech. Naomi Ruth marched in the band in Lorenzo and Ouida in the Tulia High School band, where I cheered at the Friday night sanctuary called the football field. The lights, the crowd and the hope for playoffs tickled our excitement.

If you live in Texas, you support football, or at least endure it. To explain this fact I will recall one day in the 1980s. My husband took me in his arms and said, "Twenty-three years ago today was our very first date." I was shocked and touched.

"Dickey, that is so sweet that you remembered," I said with a catch in my throat.

"Well, that was the day Tulia played Dalhart in the playoffs."

Yeah, I should have seen that one coming. Like most men, it was the football game he remembered not the first date! At least he remembered he was with me.

Even with all this background in the sport, my favorite game remains the Family Football Game.

In the Purser household—including cousins—we had enough to play two teams of six-man, and with just our family we could do four-man.

I weighed about the same as a full flour sack, the kind of sack mom used to make my dresses. And I stood taller than most kids my age. Needless to say, when we chose sides for football, I was picked last. However, my brother, Nolan, recognized my value. Long, lanky legs ran fast. No one expected me to have the ball. So Nolan named me the "Galloping Ghost." He'd hide the ball under my flour-sack dress and fake to one of my sisters as I ran to the goal line. He would even pitch me the ball and then swing me up on his shoulder. Standing over six feet tall, Nolan towered above everyone. We easily glided over the goal line.

Each year, before and several hours after Thanksgiving dinner, we chased each other up and down the yard, yelling, laughing and stumbling to victory. The last time we were all together (kids plus Mom and Dad and a ton of grandkids) we had the "monster game" in our family history. Although this time Dad was too ill to play, Mom, in her late sixties, ran to stardom. In recent years I had the joy of coaxing our cousin's family, Keith and Jan Meador, and their five kids, three daughters-in-law and ten grandkids into the family football league. Although sore and weary, they laughed and fell into an exhausted heap of joy at the end of the day.

My favorite football game took place a few years ago. Our daughters and their families came together after a long time apart. The football game was a must. We chose sides (old versus young) and the game began.

I don't remember the score. I remember my grandson, Tanner, loping across the yard and tackling his Daddy Boots and me, as we explained the rules of "touch football" once again. Granddaughter Makayla (a top finalist in the state Punt, Pass and Kick contest) passed to her cousins over her Dad's head. Then my other granddaughter, Alicia grabbed her Mom and held on until they both collapsed in laughter.

We did more than watch a game. We made memories that will replay in our minds forever.

Life Lessons: Please consider doing the same--play ball or jacks or something, all together. Push the record button on and run into the autumn sunshine. Choose sides, set boundaries, run, tumble, yell and laugh. Fall into a heap at the end of the day. Watch the sunset and make memories to last a lifetime. Play with your adult kids/grandkids, not just football and basketball. Board games, card games ... any games. It may get them farther down the field of life. Go Team!

The Christmas Doll

Christmas personifies the story of sacrificial love—God sacrificing His glory to be born in a manger so you and I might know how much He loves us. This is the reason we give gifts. Each year people all over the world give up things they want and often need so the ones they love can receive that greatly desired prize. God's gifts to us often come in perfect circles. Sometimes we wait for what seems like a lifetime to find the treasure. Even then it may appear in a way we never dreamed.

Most of my life I have searched for a Sonja Henie skating doll that I could afford like the one my sister had when she was little. When I was in second grade and deeply believed in Santa, the crops on our family farm failed. But I asked Santa for a bride doll. Mom glanced my way, her eyes reflecting a hint of sadness. I described the beautiful white gown my dream-doll would wear. Mom didn't reply. A few days later, I walked into mom's bedroom without knocking.

"Shut that door!" my mom screamed as I caught a glimpse of a cloud of white billowed over the bed and around her sewing machine. Quickly, I shut the door. I knew the rules about making your parent angry before Christmas. Santa wouldn't like it. I fell asleep that night, afraid that Santa might not find the way to my house that year.

Christmas morning we opened our stockings and found socks, candy and a pencil. My dad sat at the table with his head in a stack of bills. Mom and my siblings continued to watch me. My sister, Ouida, who was just three years older than me, shoved a box in my direction.

"It must be from Santa," Mom said. I squealed and ripped open the box—a bride doll. She was beautiful. Soft blond hair surrounded her blue eyes that blinked when I laid her down. The silk white wedding dress and the illusive veil caught on my winter-rough hands.

"Santa is real," I whispered. However, in the months ahead, I noticed Ouida's ice-skating doll no longer sat on the table by our bed. Mom never wore her white silk blouse and my sister, Ruth, no longer had two petticoats. Early in life, I found myself on the receiving end of sacrificial giving.

For a long time I wanted to find a doll like that one and give it to my sister. After her death I continued to search for one. Then out of the blue ... literally ... it came out of heaven.

The lady I had visited for the previous few years sent it. I had spent a couple of hours each week with Jo Sidener. We did a Bible study together and then I'd play my dulcimer and she and I would sing old hymns.

One day I noticed the nice doll collection that hugged the walls of her home. In the antique doll in her case was the exact Sonja Henie doll I wanted. I told Jo the story. A few months later Jo passed away. Then one day her grieving daughter dropped by and placed the doll in my hands.

"Mom knew you loved this and I want you to have it." Now the special doll brings the memories of two precious people. She sits on the table beside me, a symbol of sacrificial love.

Life Lesson: Passing on the gift of love brings a joy like nothing else. At the time you are sacrificing your time, your money or your energy, it may seem like a one-way deal. You may find excuses to back out on helping someone else, but if you do you will be backing out on the gift coming your way. The bride doll I received as a child was nothing compared to the love I discovered in the sacrificial giving. The doll I received from my neighbor did not compare to the joy I received in sharing God's word with her. Give, even when it hurts. Then wait for the joy coming your way.

The Scariest Moments

When I was five-years-old, we lived on the edge of the Caprock, outside of Ralls. On the edge of the plains, where flat-land plunges into canyons and varmints thrive, especially diamondback rattlesnakes. No matter where I played, one would eventually show up. I would hear their rattle and fear would explode from my throat as a scream. My brother Nolan often heard my cry and came running with a hoe. One of my favorite memories is of him hurtling the corral fence with a hoe in his hand. He was my hero.

Once I had to watch my cousin, "Little Dirty Face" as her mom called her. My mom and dad were helping her parents move into one of the buildings next to our house. (I use the term house loosely.) I was only five and she was a toddler, but the adults were nearby and I just had to keep her out of the driveway. We slid down the cellar door and ran down the steps into the cellar and then up the steps and slid again. On one pass, I started down the steps when I saw a huge diamond-back rattler coiled on the second step, ready to strike. I ran screaming. When I looked back, there was "Little Dirty Face" just standing there staring at the snake. It took every ounce of courage I could find in my thirty-five pound body to go get her. But my cousin was my responsibility. I pulled her to safety and waited for Nolan to respond to my cry.

Being responsible for another person's life is a scary moment. My cousin needed me; I needed my brother. He was almost the biggest one in the house at that time. And when you're the biggest, who do you call? The one bigger than you—the Heavenly Father. Call out and he will answer. With wisdom and courage and help, He will answer. Then, if you're the one responsible, you can rise to the occasion. Even if the one in need is named "Little Dirty Face" and you're only five, you can be the responsible one.

Life Lessons: In the scary moments, dial up God's phone number, JER 33:3.

> *Call to me and I will answer you and tell you great and unsearchable things you do not know.*

Listening

The world values gold and silver, but in the panhandle you learn quickly to value someone to love you, water to nourish you and trees to give you shade—in that order. Nothing survives without these three things. This story involves all three and the miracle of listening.

I won't tell you how old I was when I learned the importance of listening, because it will tend to incriminate me. Let's just say I was a tad over being a little child and a tad under being a teenager.

Children only listen on a "need to know" basis. If someone —teachers, parents, brothers or sisters—try to tell them something, it has to be something they need to know. Teachers keep you in from recess if you don't listen. Parents punish you if you don't listen. Children learn quickly which one is a "need to know" situation. If it's a sister or brother doing the talking, kids turn off their ears. Siblings offer nothing kids feel they need to know.

In the late '50s we lived on the hill out by Kaffir Switch. There's only one hill, so you will know it for sure. It has trees standing like a fort around an old farmhouse, now falling down and guarded by a herd of cows. I was tired of everyone and knew the creek was running, a perfect day for fishing.

Either mom had her fishing poles hidden or we were without one at that time. I searched for a stalk or a rod or something that would work as a fishing pole. Finally I had an idea. I found a hand saw and climbed one of the elms around the house, determined to cut me a limb perfect for fishing.

Granted, my plan was flawed. The limb I chose had to have been about ten inches around, but I was determined. As I sat about 10 or 15 feet above the ground in this tree, I began sawing ... and sawing....

My sister, Ouida, came out and yelled up at me, "Peggy, what are you doing?"

"I'm cutting a limb to make me a fishing pole."

"Get down and stop sawing on that tree. You're going to fall."

"Go away, you old heifer!" I was a sweet child.

"You are going to get hurt!"

There was really no use in her talking. My "need to know" ears were turned off.

"Okay, smartie," Ouida sat down on the porch and watched me. "Just remember, I told you so."

I kept on sawing, because she was my stupid sister. The limb swayed a little and I sawed faster. Then the limb creaked and cracked. Then the limb moved and quickly lurched downward. Then I knew what she was trying to tell me. I was sitting on the wrong end of the limb.

The limb and I crashed to the ground. Luckily, part of it clung to the tree and I slid to within four or five feet of the hard dirt underneath, then dropped the rest of the way. Ouida jumped off the porch and came running.

"Are you okay?" she asked.

"Yeah," I grumbled as I brushed off my pride and made sure nothing was broken.

Her warning words still rang in my ears. I probably shouldn't tell that story on the grounds that I might be listed in the Guinness Book of World Records as the world's only living cartoon character.

The secret of listening is a difficult lesson to learn. The miracle on this day was that I didn't break something. The other miracle is I did learn to listen to Ouida a little more often.

I think about my brothers and sisters often, rejoicing in the good times we shared. As each have passed away, I try to listen to what they learned in life that I should know—borrow a bit of their goodness to make life easier. Someone to love, water to nourish and a good shade tree—you can't beat them for happiness.

Life Lessons: Lead your children into caring for one another. Older brothers and sisters are so important in shaping their younger siblings personality, in defining who they believe they are. They shouldn't call each other, "an old heifer." Teach your children to think before they "saw." Sometimes this requires letting them fall. Tell your kids and grandkids about a day you learned a lesson and allow them time to tell you about a lesson they learned.

Little Boys and Growing Girls

Our grandson spent the first four and a half years of his life in our home. Since I was the youngest in my family and so close to the age of my nephews, this basically offered me my first experience with raising little boys. I often listen to my husband, Dickey, and his friend Johnny Barnhart talk of their childhood days which sounds a lot like an episode of Extreme Childhood Trauma. Dickey spent so many years on the farm between Kress and Tulia. That's where he met his father. He ran into the house telling his mom there was a soldier walking up to their house. Even after the war, many months of each year, he and his mom and little sister, Tanya, made the farm their home for one reason or another.

Dickey's grandparents, Draper and Mary Beaty, and their farm was a magical place for him to grow in body, mind and spirit. However, that almost didn't happen ... the growing up part was in jeopardy often.

My mother-in-law, Elizabeth, a nurse at Tulia Clinic for many years, probably began her career while nursing a wounded Dickey. She's told me of seeing him riding his tricycle up to the house with blood dripping in all directions. Then there was the day when he was about three and a half. She stood at the sink, washing dishes and looked out the window. Suddenly two little feet dangled down from the windmill. He swung back and forth on the pipe that funneled water from the windmill to the water storage tank.

Dickey and his best buddy, Johnny, took imaginative play to the extreme. Eight to ten-year-old boys can do some incredible things and live to tell the story. I heard the stories for over 48 years, but still asked Dickey to share his memories with you.

One day he and Johnny, who lived on a farm about half a mile down the road, decided to dig a cave. In this part of the county there's not even a bump in the road, so digging would be the only way to go caving. Dickey explained it this way:

"We decided to dig our cave out behind the well house. Believe it or not, after about two days of digging, we had a perfect five by five foot cave. It was about six feet deep. We even made a ladder to get down into it. This was good, but not good enough, and soon we had a perfect three by three foot tunnel that went into one side about five more feet. Next, we needed a right turn in the tunnel so we dug a three foot deep turn in the existing tunnel."

Scary? Yes. I wouldn't necessarily believe my husband; however, I verified the data with Johnny. He answered, "Yes, I think it must have been that big and I can't believe it didn't cave in." God must have had several big angels following those two around.

"When my grandfather and Mr. Barnhart saw our master piece," Dickey said, "their mouths dropped and then they covered it up much faster than it took to dig it."

Another adventure resembled a Six Flags Over Texas theme park ride before there was a Six Flags Over Texas Park.

Draper Beaty was a rig-builder in the oilfields prior to his farming days, so this one may have been in Dickey's blood.

"Johnny and I climbed to the top of the windmill and tied a block and tackle rope from the top of the windmill, out about one hundred and twenty five-feet to a telephone pole. We would then jump off holding the pulley." It may have provided a wild ride; however, I bet his mom, grandparents and several big angels shuddered at how their knots held their weight on that homemade zip line.

I believe in prayer and have used it many times in raising my girls and watching our grandchildren grow. Makayla is often mentioned for healing. From riding the dog and getting a broken arm to sliding into second base and tearing a quad muscle, she keeps me talking to the Lord. Tanner rides a skateboard...need I say more. Alicia, thank goodness, likes to read and write.

I think of the antics of childhood and know there are angels surrounding our young. We can call on those heavenly helpers, not just with the physical danger, but the physiological damage too.

Nothing proved this fact more than Dickey's motorcycle accident in 2010. He got dizzy and drove in front of a truck and hit a steel fence. He had ridden over 730,000 miles on nine different bikes without any trouble, not even a ticket. The lady behind the truck couldn't believe the truck didn't hit him. He didn't die, only broke about ten or twelve bones. Could a big angel have given him a big shove? Maybe that was the same one that tied the knots on the zip line or kept the tunnel from caving in.

Life Lessons: Pray for your family. Use the Bible to search for verses that best fit the situation and pray that verse over the loved one or friend. No matter the circumstance, keep believing: God is who He says He is and He will do what the Bible says he will do. Pray especially hard for the little boys of all ages.

The Luckiest Girl on Dip Street and Her Dad

Ann Wallace Hooks, the luckiest girl on Dip Street (I call her that because her bedroom window overlooked the red-brick phenomenon.) recently reminded me of the "fine art of dragging Dip."

"There's an 'art' to driving down Dip Street," Ann explained. "You have to veer to the right at the end of each block. If you don't, you will bottom out your car on the real dip. It's a true art to take those dips without harming your car."

I add to Ann's directions the details on how to make a U-turn without power-steering, while holding a cup full of icy-cold Dr. Pepper. If you put the cup between your teeth to turn the wheel with both hands, don't talk. This is just one of those things I learned on Dip Street. It was a "cold" fact of life for a sixteen-year-old to comprehend.

My life on Dip Street began in fifth grade when I was stuffed in the back seat and forced to hide if my sister and her best friend, Lana, drove past any boys. Then I met Ann who moved to town about the same time as I did. We could see Dip Street from her window and on a cool summer night, the sounds of laughter and "hollering" swirled up to the window and drew a sigh of "will I ever be old enough to drive?"

It was yelling, not texting, on the drag back then. Peter, the 1961 foreign exchange student from Denmark, wrote recently, "I remember crazy rides down Dip Street—and the first time I was told to *holler*, 'Move that heap!' to a neighboring driver."

Ann also had a canopy bed, the first one I had ever seen. Her dad built a wall at the end of the bed and then hand-cut a curved part for the sides attached to the ceiling. Her mom made everything: bedspread, curtains and the most amazing dresses. I thought for many years, that Ann was extremely rich because things would show up in a fashion magazine or the dress shop downtown and then Ann would have one. And Ann's mom served avocados, plus all kinds of exotic foods we didn't grow on the farm. It never seemed strange to me that Ann and her family lived above the funeral home. Her dad, the funeral director, always wore a suit and the perfect smile for each of life's occasions.

There were times when Dip Street became a place of, "Did you hear, the news?" Someone would roll down their window. "Billy Bob and Suzie Q" are getting married. Couples got married back in the day. Most often the news was about a victory in football, basketball, band, drama, choir, and from Ann's window we heard it first, even if we weren't old enough to drive.

Then there were times we heard the worst news. "Did you hear? He got killed." Fathers, farmers, firemen, teenagers-moms, and people going over railroad tracks too late. Young adults who would never be old adults. Their lives evaporated like raindrops on the hood of an overheated car.

When death reached into our happy days and jerked us into reality, Ann's dad was there with a gentle smile that understood and helped. The funeral home stood close to the Methodist, Baptist and Presbyterian churches, just west of the courthouse and down the road from the hospital.

Back in the day, funeral homes were built in the center of town. Like birth, death was a central part of life. Death wasn't removed, sanitized and covered over then. It was another stage of being. Men like Mr. Wallace helped more than the preacher's lofty words. They did the work of life. Death affected us all, but it was easier with friends. Parents, teachers and coaches in our small community taught us how to handle the bumps in the road, and showed us the promise of heaven

Life Lessons: Teach your children that the journey is about learning how to take the bumps, accepting the stages of life and having friends there to help. Most importantly, knowing where you will be at the end of the road.

Liar, Liar

The first time I met the guy at the swimming pool, I didn't know he would change my life. He oozed muscles and dripped handsome all over the lifeguard stand. When my sister, Ouida, and I entered, she stopped to pay, but I just walked in as if I weren't twelve-years-old. The lifeguard raised one eyebrow and grinned at me.

"Are you sure you're only ?" he asked.

I nodded sheepishly, afraid he would guess the truth. I was just too poor to pay. Visiting our older sister, Ruth, for the summer, we spent our days at the pool and our evenings at church youth activities. Every time I passed the cute lifeguard, I had to act eleven, while my sixteen-year-old sister flirted non-stop.

The problem was further complicated at church. To be in the youth department, I had to be thirteen. It seemed only fair to me that if I smudged the truth to go swimming, I should at least smudge the truth to go to church.

The fun times rolled all summer until the church youth retreat. I had left the cabin, heading for the dining room, when I saw him.

"Oh, no!" I cried and pointed at him as if he were death itself. "The lifeguard from the city pool." Heat burned my face. "What's he doing here?"

"Wonderful!" Ouida squealed.

"He'll know I lied." I whispered in humiliation.

"He won't even remember you, Twerp."

41

"I can't go in there." I turned and went behind a row of trees.

"You'll miss supper," Ouida said as she rushed into the dining hall.

I hid in the trees and hoped he would leave soon.

"Peggy," Ouida called through the trees. "He's staying the entire weekend. He's one of the youth leaders. You'll have to see him sooner or later."

"No, I can't." Tears flooded my eyes. A slice of shame lumped in my throat. Darkness crept across camp as singing and laughter floated through the night air. I missed the warmth of the fellowship. But liars didn't belong in the church youth group. I was a liar.

"Peggy." The deep voice calling through the trees shook me as if it were the voice of God. "Peggy," the lifeguard called louder.

"Yes," I whispered.

"Hey, sweetheart," he sat down on the log beside me. "Why are you hiding from me?"

"I lied."

"Yeah, I know." He tugged on my ponytail. "I forgive you."

"How can you forgive me? I'm nothing but a liar."

"The Bible says, 'forgives us our trespasses as we forgive those who trespass against us.'"

"I am so sorry," I cried. "I won't ever go swimming again unless I can pay."

"Then it's forgotten. Let's go eat." He squeezed my shoulder.

"But ... there's more. I'm really too young to be in youth. I'm twelve. I lied to the preacher. I wish everyone was as eager to get into church as you are." He stood up and took my hand. "Well, let's go in and tell him. He has a very big heart. I bet he'll forgive you too."

He did.

Life Lessons: When you tell your children about your own mistakes and past sins, it gives them the courage to tell you about their own.

"Liar, Liar" was originally printed in *Chicken Soup for the Soul: Teens Talk Middle School.*

The Miracle of…

Looking Your Best

Don Beaty and his daughter, Deedee, were two of a kind. Don was a sailor and served in World War II. He returned to the U.S. and married a darling little lady named Cootie. Actually that's not her name but few people know her real name. Don became a welder and then farmed just north of Kress. He did many things in life, but he was always a scholar.

Deedee was Don and Cootie's youngest daughter and one of the best teachers I've ever known. She pulled many kids out of the pit of failure. Deedee grew up on the farm in Kress. Daddy's girl was probably the name she loved best. If Don allowed, it she would be his shadow, staying by his side all day long. She loved lunch and dinner when her daddy came home from the fields.

"Rub my back, Deedee." Don would stretch out before the TV and fall asleep watching the noon news while she rubbed his back or his temples or just snuggled up beside him. This became their special time.

When she turned ten, Deedee discovered her mom's makeup and loved how the bright colors could change a face. So one day at lunchtime, while Don slept, Deedee applied a generous helping of makeup to her daddy's face.

After Don woke up, he mumbled, "See ya later." Then he slapped his old, oil-stained hat on his head and headed out the door. He jumped into his dilapidated pickup-truck and headed to Larson's restaurant in downtown Kress. All the farmers met at Larson's Café shortly after lunch for coffee, a weather report and the news from the city.

"Gee, Don, you sure look nice!" One friend said with a snicker as Don sauntered across the room. Several others chuckled or hid their smiles behind work-worn hands as Don moved past them and slid into a chair.

Why were they laughing? He puzzled and tried to ignore them because they were farmers with little to entertain them. Pretty soon the room was a-buzz with laughter, everyone pointing toward Don. After a few rude comments that he didn't understand at all, he decided the bugs and rattlesnakes back at the farm would be more polite company. He grabbed his hat and took off toward his truck. As he opened the door and slid in, he noticed a strange reflection in his review mirror. A closer look revealed bright blue eye-shadow, hot pink lips and rosy cheeks.

"Deedee!" he yelled at the wind. "I'm gonna get you, girl."

Deedee Beaty, my husband's cousin, first told me this story shortly before her father passed away. Later, as a children's author, I visited her classroom in Kress. She and her students had transformed the classroom into a log cabin just for me and my book. We were doing a writing exercise where we told something funny that had happened in our life. She told this tale of make-up fun with her rich, wonderful laughter that delighted her students and opened up their souls to learning.

I hoped she would write the story down or record it in some way. It has become one of my favorite family stories. However, too soon Deedee's life as an amazing teacher, daughter, mom, Nana and friend was cut short by breast cancer. One day before she died, I called and asked her to tell me the story once again while I typed it. We only made it half way through before she had to rest. It was okay because I remembered the story very well. I have told the story at almost every school I visit as an author.

One of my goals has become to encourage people to write or record their family stories like this one, stories that tie a family's past and future together with cords of laughter and bonds of love. It will be truly sad if our time on earth is defined only by music lyrics, a sitcom and other TV shows.

Life Lessons: Make time to tell stories. Turn off the TV or the radio; talk and listen with your kids. I know I've said this before, but this is one of the most important events of your day and it will shape their life, define who they are. In the past the dinner table did more than hold books, keys, bills, or various lost items, it offered a place to nourish the body. It provided an opportunity to nourish the soul and pass down oral history.

The Miracle of...

Watermelons

Summer ending, school beginning, long hot bus rides home, and watermelons—juicy, ripe, busted open and dug out by the handfuls, running down your chin in rivers of sweetness. Memories of growing up on the farm remain as sweet.

Back then, my ride home on the school bus, out to Kaffir Switch and up to the hill, took about forty-five minutes to an hour. It was hot and bone-rattling bumpy. However, the ride gave me time to laugh, talk to friends, get into trouble. At home, I ran in, grabbed a snack, changed out of my dress. (Back then we weren't allowed to wear slacks or jeans to school.) I would dash out the door and jump into the irrigation-well pool. Cold doesn't define that water. Icy water blew out of a huge pipe and created this amazing white sand pool, eight-feet or so in diameter.

We worked until sundown everyday finishing up canning and freezing our winter food from our garden. That garden ran the length of our road which was half a section long. It took forever to hoe to the end of a row and get behind the corn where mom couldn't see us. There we would search for a watermelon that was ripe. The skill of detecting a ripe melon requires a finely tuned ear and great thumping skills. Outsmarting my mom about how many melons were still on the vine was the difficult part. We did use the hoe...to bury the rind. By late summer, she lost count. Before the first freeze, we had to pick all the melons, put them in the barn and cover them in hay.

As the Dog Days of Summer turned into crisp autumn, we pulled cotton after school. The day ended with a huge piece of cold watermelon and seconds if we wanted. The treasured, red juicy orbs of early summer were so plentiful by fall that we soon took the taste for granted. Wintertime has a way of making everything better. We ran out of tasty canned goods by February and had to eat spinach and greens until summer. With the garden planted in early spring, we anticipated how wonderful the first watermelons would be. Now modern technology brings us fresh produce all year, but none are as good as the ones picked on the farm when I was a child. Few things remain as good as the memory of the watermelons we devoured behind the corn.

WARNING! Items in your rearview mirror may appear to be larger, sweeter and better than they truly were.

Nothing is like it used to be--including my own reflection. Recently this truth came to mind as I read a conversation from a few people about going back home. "It isn't what it used to be."

No, my hometown isn't what it used to be. Neither is Dallas or New York City. Believe me, those cities are truly depressing. Looking in the mirror, I see I'm not what I used to be. Actually, there is a great deal more of me, more pounds, wrinkles and gray hair. But if I look through God's eyes, I see someone who is the same on the inside and yet wiser and more loving.

If we are always looking at what used to be, we will be disappointed. If we look at the present with hope and trust in our neighbors, we get a glimpse of a bright future, a memory in the making--helping one another through life.

Life Lessons: Remembering the good old days can be a blessing. Enjoy today. Pass down the art of canning or making jelly and jam. Visit a farm. Hug a farmer. Thump a watermelon.

Diving into Reality

When we moved to Tulia, my father told us of the two-story mansion with a mile long yard, an orchard, a stream and a swimming pool. Yes, the house did have two stories ... there was an attic. It was on the hill between Tulia and Happy. I'm sure mansion was the right word in the 1890s when it was built, but not in 1957.

When the wind blew from the north the kitchen cabinet doors opened. The yard was a wheat field. The stream, we discovered, was an irrigation ditch and the pool turned out to be the huge sandy pit formed where the well drew the water up through the six inch pipe and sprayed it four feet out. I still remember how cold, clear and wonderful it was to swim there. The orchard was a few apricot trees between our house and the Hansen's farm, down on the main road out of Kaffir Switch. Nothing will ever taste as good as those apricots.

When my sister, Naomi Ruth, accepted her first date in Tulia, the poor boy fell through the porch of the "mansion." This house at one time had been a grand place, but that was about sixty or seventy years before our arrival. Mom made it home, just as she did all the other places we had lived. Daddy repaired the porch. He planted crops in a time when cotton grew as high as a farmer dreams.

Swimming offered a rare treat and not because of the irrigation well. The parks in Lubbock and Amarillo, where my family often convened to make homemade ice cream, featured huge pools. And the city pool in Tulia definitely delighted us.

Having quickly grown taller in fifth and sixth grade, I couldn't wear my swimsuit. It was too short by about a foot or two. So I borrowed my sister's. It was a little big at the top and the bottom. When I dove into the water, the top cups of the suit dented in where I should have dented out, but didn't. This was totally embarrassing. But I'm creative!

I rushed into the dressing room, rolled up toilet paper and stuffed it into each cup. Perfect! Then I rushed out to enjoy swimming. I dove in ready to impress everyone. Not only did the cups still dent in, but the white soggy paper floated all around me. I didn't say I was too bright in junior high; I said I was creative.

One of the first times I remember diving into that cool water, washing away the hot, taught me a lesson most of us have to learn sometime in life. Pretending to be something you aren't never works. Accepting who you are, how you look and even how smart you are...or are not...works best. Just face the problem, work to correct it and laugh at yourself a little along the way.

Life Lessons: When you share a story from your past, it teaches your children and grandchildren to take life's embarrassments and turn them into laughter. It also assures them that they will live through those times just as you did. Laughter lengthens your lifespan, too. Learn to laugh.

Hiding in the Back Seat

If you're too young to drive down Dip Street, the next best thing is riding in the backseat.

"Okay, Twit," Ouida would say as we jumped into the car with one of her best friends. "Stay down and if we stop to talk to boys, you hide and do not let anyone see you."

"Why?" I asked. "Your friends all like me."

"Because no one drags Dip Street with their little sister. Just be glad I let you ride around with us," she said, as if I didn't know she had no choice. If she took me home, she would have to stay at home, too.

Retribution came at the drive-in theater. Being younger I could get in to the Drive-in free. If my sister Ruth drove, she had to pay for a ticket. That left Ouida to be the one to hide in the backseat, so we could afford the movie. I loved it.

Life Lessons: Paybacks are the pits. There is always retribution.

The Miracle of...

Driving Down Dip Street
The Teen Years

How to be Popular ... or Not

The one thing I wanted desperately, as a pre-teen, was to be popular. I thought being popular would prove my value. All the love I didn't receive, all the pain, I stuffed down deep. I hid my sadness and said, "Okay, I'm not a good person, but if I become popular and enough people like me, then maybe others will think I'm a good person." However, the problem continued. I wasn't popular and the harder I tried, the more the other kids pulled away from me.

Then I discovered the amazing secret. God loves me just as I am.

Wow! That was a news flash for me. I didn't like me, so how could God love me? But there it was in black and white in the HOLY Bible. Not only was it a holy Bible, it had once belonged to a king named James. Until that moment I thought I had to be good enough to earn God's love. The Pastor showed me I didn't; it was a free gift. All I had to do was accept and believe it. I also found a group of people who loved me in the church in my hometown.

This took me on a journey—the journey of looking at others and asking, "Do they know they are loved?" I found people who would listen as I shared my darkest pain and others who needed to talk. Somewhere in the next two years, between ninth grade and eleventh grade, a miracle happened —I chose to like other people, because God loves them just as they are. In the process, I found I liked myself.

Then one day the principal announced the outcome of the try-outs for varsity cheerleader. I had always tried out, knowing I'd never make it because it was all popular votes.

"There's a tie," he said over the loudspeaker and I was one of the girls in the runoff. My friends in English class patted me on the back. A haze of disbelief blocked the reality of the moment. The principal's voice boomed through the speaker. "We'll have a runoff election Monday."

The next week I still felt confused. The other girl was popular. What was I doing with her in a runoff? It got more unbelievable--I won!

As the week continued I discovered I had so many classmates that were truly happy I won. The choir kids, the drama team and the volleyball team. Even the kids in my classes that didn't belong to a group, those that smiled at me each day, they all congratulated me. It slowly dawned on me that they liked me because I liked them. No longer did I pretend to like people to gain their favor. No longer was I pretending to like myself. I felt a real love for them, a love God had given to me.

Maybe that was the moment I realized the universal truth —popularity does not exist outside of high school. It is a paranormal phenomenon concocted by young girls and their mothers who were once teenage girls.

When a person realizes popularity and fame aren't real, they discover friendship. They choose to be around the people they like.

Life Lesson: Share with your kids the popularity myth, and don't leave out your feelings of being popular ... or not.

Where's the Drag?

Many Texas towns in the happy days era had a drag. In Amarillo, instead of Dip Street it was Polk Street. My husband, Dickey (1961 red Corvette), and his friends drove around Stanley's, Dino's or Twings.

My niece, Susie Sims, tells me that in Houston in the 70s Spring Branch High's drag was Long Point. In the 80s her brother, Brandon, reports they cruised the curve, or the Westheimer curve. And the best-known drag anywhere is probably Galveston's famous Strand.

Texas isn't the only state where the social drag reigns. Perfect places to cruise thrive. My friends shared: Pamela Schoenfeld Stapleton said, "In Visalia, California, the drag was Mooney Blvd." Brian Muerhead said, "Fremont Street was the place to be in Las Vegas, Nevada, before it was enclosed and made into a mall." And Bob Cook (an award-winning artist whose works often include vintage cars) said, "We used to cruise Main St. down to Winsteads on the Plaza, then over to NU-Way Drive-In on Troost Street in Kansas City."

In Yellville, Arkansas, the young people called it "Scooping the Loop. "We started at the Hilltop Drive-In, which was appropriately located at the top of the hill, and went down Church Street past the town square," Marcy Carter Lovick explains. "At the Dairy (something off brand) drive-in, we made a right turn, went one block and made a second right at Dr. Kelly's office to go back up the hill on a parallel street." Marcy is now a leader in the Texas Daughters of the American Revolution and other historical groups. She is a tremendous help in locating family tree records as well as "scooping the loop."

Other writing friends recently shared their memories. Connie Leonard says, "In Albuquerque, New Mexico, we cruised Central, around Vip's Big Boy." Margo Carmichael says, "The Main in Palafox Street in Pensacola, Florida" was the place to be seen back in the day. Robert Taylor cruised 7th Street in Fort Worth. Patricia Moore says, "Cooper Street in Arlington, was the drag."

My nephews Scott, Marcus and Adam Eiland, spent their teen years in New Providence, New Jersey, cruising up and down Route 22. Marcus is a Young Life leader, therefore he is still draggin' Route 22.

Jan Meador added, "My kids cruised on 23rd Street in Canyon, which was Highway 87. They circled McDonald's and then Sonic. I always felt badly because it wasn't a *Dip Street*."

Although these memories of our teen years may warm our hearts, the same scenes brought us fear and trembling when our kids were teenagers. The main drag in Burleson was called "cruising the square." My daughter, Cynthia, and her friend, Mikki Lee, spent a lot of time driving around Dalton's corner, trying to decide if there were more cute boys inside or outside. When I thought my daughter was cruising Highway 67 in Cleburne with Jennifer Greeson, they were cruising Camp Bowie Boulevard in Fort Worth.

Our oldest daughter felt slighted in cruisin' time. We lived in the DFW area and were very careful with our first-born. Plus she was five-foot-one and a 38-22-34 knock-out at fifteen. We didn't let her out of our sight any more than we had to. I do believe she squeezed in a cruise down Cooper Street in Arlington several times, in between cheerleading and youth group.

Perhaps the difference in a city and a small town drag is really about freedom. Freedom is easier in a less crowded place.

Life Lessons: No matter where you drag, enjoy the ride.

Walking the Halls of High School

I'm not sure where the cavemen satisfied their longing for social networking. Perhaps they meandered around the watering hole in between hunts, smiling shyly at the cavewomen. They probably talked about their latest set of round rocks and planned on racing them back to the cave. And maybe the cavewomen gossiped about who had a date to the cave-prom. The caveteachers probably stood nearby and checked the cavegirls' saber-tooth-tiger fur to make sure they were the proper length to wear to school.

The Romans met at the coliseum, kicked the wheels on the chariot and talked about how much horsepower they owned. In the 1800s, the French promenaded in the park on Sunday afternoons and ladies checked out who had the biggest hat.

But in Tulia, Texas, in the '50s and '60s, it was about driving up and down Dip Street in the latest hotrod and walking the halls at Tulia High School. My teen years were a blessed time. I imagine everyone thinks that, but the '50s and '60s were truly the wonder-years, because regular gas was fifty-cents a gallon.

Fifty-cent gas sparked the engines on everything from a VW bug, Chevy Impala, and Ford Falcon, to a Pontiac GTO or LeMans. If you were really lucky, you got to drive an El Camino pickup truck. I'm not sure lucky is the right word, but it did get me up and down Dip Street. It didn't run on propane like my friend's white Buick did. Her father was a man before his time.

Walking the halls at THS was also a craft. Like taking the dips on Dip Street, you had to know how to walk from your locker and to the front hallway, by way of your latest heartthrob's locker, without anyone noticing. Most importantly, you had to avoid the homemaking classes. The homemaking teacher would be there, with her yardstick, measuring the distance between the hem of your dress/skirt and the floor. It didn't matter how tall you were. Your skirt had to be a modest distance from the floor.

Walking the hall also promoted relationships and acceptance, judgment and condemnation. There may have been a little sharing of homework too. Conversations went something like this:

"I have on seven petticoats. How many do you have on?" "Love your new hoop skirt." Or maybe, "Do you use Aquanet to get your hair that big and backcombed?" "Do you have a clippie I can borrow?" "What questions are on the science test?"

I hope the schools today allow walking in the hall, passing your latest heartthrob's, (excuse me crush's) locker. Today "texting," "posting," "snapping," "tweeting," and all other "ings" make up the social setting for teens to build relationships. Just like "driving" down the drag or "walking" the hallway, it is a place to meet or break up with the love of your life, build up your friends or ... tear them down.

Some think that electronic social media is much more difficult for kids to survive. Rumors make the rounds a little faster and mean comments are heard by more than a whisper in the hallway. However, there is an electronic path back to the person saying the mean things. It's easier to stand up for kind acts and stop mean ones. Unfortunately, the world-wide-web is just that ... worldwide, and it lasts forever. Like the unseen spider web, a young person can get trapped there and devoured by the enemy.

Like the caveman's watering hole, it could be a life-or-death place where you should watch carefully and always be on the lookout for predators. Meeting the wrong person or giving out too much information is a very real problem for our young people.

I remember back in the day being accepted by your peers or your teachers was a tough balancing act. Even more difficult was driving fast enough to impress your friends and slow enough for the policeman waiting just off the main drag.

Recently, I was in on a discussion on social media (Yes, even old people go there.) about cars and someone said, "In the old-days, guys were defined by the cars they drove. "How fast will it go?" "Do you have four-on-the-floor?" "Bucket seats?"

I admit it; I accepted my first date with Dickey Freeman partly because he drove a red Corvette. He sold it just before our first date and picked me up in a plain Chevrolet. I still married him.

Sheet metal, leather, plastic and rubber don't make the man. It wasn't the hotrods the cool chicks sought on Dip Street. Teenagers through time have searched for one thing—relationship—being accepted. It doesn't matter if you're driving the drag or walking the halls, texting or tweeting. Being accepted is on your mind.

Life Lessons: Relax! No matter what you wear or what you drive, you are accepted. You are worth all the rubies, sapphires and golden streets in heaven. The Creator of the universe left it all and came to earth for you. He chose to be born in a stinking stable, work as a poor carpenter, walk for hundreds of miles and listen to people's problems endlessly. All of this and then they nailed spikes into his hands and hung him on a cross. And when he died you and I were on his mind. We are more than accepted; we are redeemed.

The Cross at Ceta Canyon – Real Love

My first visit to Ceta Canyon took place in 1959. As an eighth grader and in my BC (Before Christ) days, the luminous cross that shines across the canyons didn't speak to me. I really don't remember it from that time. Nor do I remember any sermons or lessons from camp that first summer. I do remember Timmy B! Didn't every girl in the panhandle of Texas remember him? I remember feeling sorry for my friend because she was his cousin and therefore would never be able to marry him. I, however, was not related. Therefore our wedded-bliss was assured. I don't think Timmy was aware of our marriage predestination. Besides he was a Methodist, not a Presbyterian. I was neither. If there had been a church of boy-crazy, I would have joined immediately.

The cross may have been as beautiful in 1959 as it was in 1960, but I was spiritually blind and could not see. I was spiritually deaf and could not hear, a lot like a teenager when their parent speaks.That winter brought more than a blizzard. God's spirit flooded over many adults and young people in my hometown that year. I was one of those blessed. I found real love.

After that amazing spiritual awakening, we returned to Ceta Canyon for a retreat. I had accepted God's love, Christ's sacrifice for me. Now I knew. I saw. I heard. There was forgiveness and power to change.

That didn't mean I was suddenly perfect. I still often acted unloving, holier-than-thou and may have told a fib or two. I still drove our youth sponsor, Delbert Devin, crazy. Along with several other girls who went on retreat to Ceta Canyon, I tried to sneak out of the cabin each night. On one trip I remember in particular, Betty Devin, "the sleepless counselor'" kept one eye open all weekend. God is so good to send men and women of wisdom and love to young foolish girls.

On this trip, although I still did dumb things and felt insecure, I now SAW the cross. I understood its meaning. A vertical beam reaching from God to ME, it stood as a way God could explain to me the depth of His love. He loved me so much that He was not only willing to die for me ... He sent His Son to die for me. How can that be? That fact changed me forever. There are many people who might die to save me, but who would send their child to die so that I could live, understanding how much I am loved?

In the next few years, God blessed many of us in several different churches. As we grew, we learned about the horizontal beam of the cross. On this crossbeam Jesus stretched out His arms to hug us. Therefore, we stretch out our arms to hug others.A great book to read while walking through the valley of the little c. Connie Lewis Leonard is an excellent writer and handles a tough topic. This story will help family members of cancer victims understand and yet still entertain them with a heartfelt story of family love.

In those few short years, our community gave the world a half-dozen preachers, a few preacher's wives and several missionaries. Because of that cross, and many others--some lit, some rugged and gnarled—all pointing to God's amazing grace, we have the best gift ever.

All crosses hold a special place in my heart, but that cross, shining across the canyon, represents the chasm of life—shining to reveal the gaping holes of our pain and hurt. When the light of the cross lights our pathway to healing, we finally see. And we also see the pain of others. We find we can become a healing friend, neighbor or light to the world.

Life Lessons: Take every opportunity to talk about the cross of Christ with your kids. Help them understand it's not just jewelry or a big sign at the church ... it's a valentine. Each cross is a valentine to you from God.

The "Other" Side of Town

Christmas in the panhandle of Texas offers a wide variety of weather—cold and colder. On this particular day, it did like it often does; it turned cold, then colder. We gathered at the church youth building and prepared boxes to take to the underprivileged. I was fourteen and very young on my faith walk. This event hit me in a resentful part of my gut that I didn't visit often.

"Hey, God! I'm the poor one here. My friends have new dresses and mouton coats. Yes, a mouton fur only looks like beaver or seal. It's actually sheepskin, but it ruled the formal fashion world and all my friends had one. Well maybe not all, God. But I'm tired of having nothing and wanting to do all the things my friends do."

That afternoon as we left the church and headed to the "other" side of town, the usually glorious sunset of bold pink and orange muted into gray storm clouds that carried a promise of snow. The food boxes had to be unloaded at the church on the "poor" side of town and then carried to each home.

My family passed this community from time to time. This was literally on the other side of the tracks from the nice part of town. It was an alternate route to the farm my dad leased. But I had never been up into its narrow, dark dirt roads. Its shacks and sheds appeared like a maze as we bounced toward the lone church near the center of the slums.

The pastor greeted us with his beautiful smile and we rushed in to be Santa for these unknown people. A friend and I grabbed a box with handwritten directions on the top. Why didn't they just give us the address?

Soon we realized there were no addresses. We quickly followed the note to the last house on the second row. But it wasn't a house. It was someone's shed. I timidly knocked on the thin door. It slowly opened, more by the force of the wind than anything.

"Come on in," a voice called. We stepped in and closed the door. A room the size of a small bathroom stood bare of anything but a table, two chairs, and an old black stove with a pipe up to the roof. No ceiling—just two by four inch beams and plywood. No floor—just dirt—cold, hard, Panhandle dirt. A toddler sat on the ground in a diaper and a small shirt. Suddenly, not having a mouton coat for Christmas seemed silly. This baby needed shoes, warm clothes and probably food.

"Hello," I called to the person moving on the other side of the small divider. "We brought you a gift from our church."

"Thank you, I sure can use that," a young voice answered.

I bent down to pick up the toddler. "What's the baby's name?"

"That's Billy and this is…" The mom walked in with a younger baby on her hip. I looked up and quickly recognized her. It was Sarah Jane. She had been in my class two years before in seventh grade. Sarah Jane, the best junior high basketball player who made much better grades in math than I did, stood before me, obviously upset and embarrassed. I smiled. We quickly opened the box and showed her the food and toys for the babies.

"Your babies are darling," I stammered and my friend added comments. None of what we said seemed important. This was a girl our age—a former classmate. As we left, a man twice her age stumbled by, reeking of liquor.

The walk back to the church seemed much longer than it did from the church earlier. We didn't say much. The dirt road squished under our shoes with something I didn't want to know about. And the drive home that night was far too short--a few miles to my home, a small frame house on Floyd Street, not the big fine houses where my friends lived. But it had floors and carpet. It had a heater and a nice comfy sofa.

In January I would go back to school and laugh with my friends, play basketball and perform in plays. However, I would never complain about being poor again. I was rich, richer than before I took those gifts that night—before I received the gift of appreciation.

No matter how poor we think we might be, there is someone in worse circumstances. God's plan is for us to share through our church and our community--to celebrate Jesus' birthday by gifting to those in need. We give--not out of abundance but out of what we have, no matter how small we think it is.

I did get a fur coat that Christmas. It wasn't mouton. It was fake fur. Today I'd be in perfect style; in 1960 I was perfectly warm.

Life Lessons: Teach your children to love giving. Don't tell them about it; let them experience the joy of giving to those in need. No matter how poor they think they are, find a child somewhere in the world and share what little you have. It's best if the giving is in person--an old folks home, a children's hospital, a church in a poor neighborhood. It's the best gift you will give them.

Dating

In the last fifty years, many things have changed; however, none more than the high cost of living and the practice of dating. Gas has gone from 50 cents a gallon to 3.50 plus today. A burger and fries soared from $1.00 to $8.00. The high cost of dating concerns me even more than the pain at the pump or the local burger joint.

As a teen, I dated over one hundred different boys from the time I was sixteen until I married at nineteen. Today if someone said they dated 125 different guys in three years, their morals would be greatly questioned. I don't see teens having fun on dates. They seem to get bored quickly and slip into the trials of marriage before they are officially married. We had fun--crazy, falling in love or "like" fun. I've been thinking about all those dates, the friendships and life-time relationships that developed.

One date occurred on a Saturday morning. As we drove around and talked about school, the football game the night before, we drove out to Tule Lake. It was a beautiful day and, believe it or not, the dam spillway overflowed. I don't remember that happening many times.

"Let's go fishing," my date said as he pulled up near the dam.

"We don't have any fishing poles," I answered.

"Haven't you ever caught fish with your hands?"

I laughed, while he waded into the stream and began watching for fish. Then he suddenly flipped one on the bank. A little mud-cat flopped and wiggled in the sunlight and finally grew still. I quickly joined my date on the slick spillway. Mud squeezed up between my toes. I stared ahead and watched for fish.

My date explained, "When you see the fish a few feet in front of you, start to close your hands or you'll miss it."

I don't think I've ever had more honest to goodness fun on a date. We scooped fish up and tossed them on the bank, and then we took them by a few places where we knew people might be hungry. In 1963 I had three dates in one day. This shocked me since I wasn't allowed to car-date until I turned sixteen and, sadly, not many boys called even after I turned sixteen. Dates included: going to Picnic (our hometown equivalent of Old Settlers Reunion), a Sadie Hawkins/twerp date, the Dairy Queen, and, of course, driving up and down Dip Street.

Once there was a triple date (six of us) and we laughed all night. Another time a group of us took a picnic to Ceta Canyon and went hiking. I got kissed under the Third Falls. That boy remains a dear friend to my husband and me. We even had dates to youth meetings and revivals.

In the '50s and '60s, we had four or five formal affairs to attend each year. These memories swirl like sweet, long-lasting candy. Girls floated across the gym or cafeteria like multi-colored clouds. Boys wore white sports coats, suits or a nice shirt and tie.

One of my other favorite dates also included fishing. My mom and my brother joined me and my date as we went fishing on a private lake near Amarillo. We were rigged to catch crappie--a rig on our line that had two hooks. My brother caught a huge fish that broke his line and got away. To my mom, that was the worst thing that could happen. As my brother tied on new hooks, my date caught a monster. He worked and worked to get it to the boat and mom got the net. It was actually two huge fish and he had also caught the line my brother lost. That line also had two huge crappies on it.

My mom laughed and said, "He caught four fish at once! Peggy, you can marry this one." I did!

The high cost of dating today has nothing to do with the cost of a movie or burgers and cokes. The moral fiber of our youth has been depleted. Even the very best kids are assaulted by peer pressure to skip the dating process where you take a year or two to test your feelings and build a relationship. They are convinced by songs, movies and society that physical intimacy is not about relationship. The world shouts over the parents' whispers. Turning the volume down on the world's morality and protecting your preteens and teenagers has become mandatory. Prayer and going to church as a family helps.

Life Lessons: Keep your kids closer, reminding them of the value of relationships built through time without physical intimacy. Demand group dating. Sixteen, or the end of the sophomore year, is a good guideline for one-on-one car dating. The most important thing you can do for teens in the community is give them options. Provide activities and events where dating is fun, not life-altering.

Cruisin' USA

Like my cousin, Jan Doan Meador, says, "Did anyone ever leave their house for anything without making at least one drag down Dip Street?" Me? Every last time! Thank gosh, my Ma and Dado just lived one block off Dip Street. I could always make at LEAST one or two drags coming and going.

Only in Texas, a Dip Street story (last names avoided for a reason). Tim tells it this way, "Gary and I were riding down Dip Street on our horses and some young kid was riding his bicycle in and out between cars, causing a ruckus among the people that parked in the middle talking to one another. Gary and I told him to get out of there. The kid made some "remarks"...so we decided to chase him off, but changed our minds and roped him. Problem solved!"

Some guys circled the monument in the middle of Dip Street 32 times just to see if they could.

The sweetest stories are the best. "I met Glenda there. Then one day, driving east on Dip Street from the west end, near the park, I told Glenda to look in the glove box. She did and there was her engagement ring. We married in August of 1959. The marriage lasted fifty-four years, seven months and seven days." - Dwight Stevens (Glenda died a few weeks before Dwight shared this story.

Life Lessons: Precious moments add up to a lifetime.

A Man Named Papa

When I met Papa, aka Delbert Devin, God's right-hand-man in the task of shepherding the youth of my hometown church for almost forty years, he farmed six days a week and then volunteered to listen to us cry on his off-time. (I say that as if farmers have an off-time.) He got us out of trouble, then poked and prodded to keep us on the right path. In the middle of teaching us to love God's word, he organized us into teams and we traveled over the Texas plains singing, preaching and sharing our faith with others.

Fifty years later, on a Sunday after Picnic, I joined hands with ten or so of those same friends whose lives had also been blessed by Papa's huge spirit. There were pastors, teachers, missionaries, farmers, writers, editors, and Peter, the boy who came from Denmark to find a deeper spiritual life and share it with all of us. We sang the songs Papa taught us and prayed that his journey to the afterlife would be peaceful, knowing that as we said goodbye, heaven was brightened by his wonderful smile.

Delbert Devin was a miracle in my life. He loved me and hundreds of other kids in Swisher County and beyond. Just a farmer, who volunteered his life to love like Jesus did. Delbert and his precious wife, Betty, didn't have time to share their life with us. They didn't have the money for gas or to leave their jobs. They had a family who had needs. But they made time, used less and gave up themselves for young people who needed love.

We could praise this wonderful man and say a well-deserved prayer over his grave. However, because we'd had him or someone like him in our lives, we had to do more.

As we stood around the bed and sang a song for Papa, I remembered a song that asks, "When I come to the end of life's weary road, who will sing one song for me?" Who will sing a song for me? Who will sing a song for you?

Life Lessons: In your church, neighborhood or on your street, there's a young person needing to hear that God loves them. It's the Baby Boomer generation's time to answer that call. If every one of us selected just one young person to love and encourage, imagine how many future preachers, teachers, authors, editors, missionaries, and farmers will volunteer to pass love on to the next generation.

The Eagle and the Crow

Eagles are amazing. We think of them as strong, powerful and never to be bullied. But even the strong and powerful suffer from being bullied. Crows are small and not at all strong. They can be frightened away with the slightest leaves rustling in the wind. Yet crows will attack an eagle. Oftentimes they come in a mob and go after the eagle from behind.

Much like a bunch of fifth graders, a high school group, or a gaggle of mean old women, this mob of crows won't stop. If the eagle turns to face them they dart away only to return when the eagle isn't watching. They nip and dive at the eagle and, unlike the owl, the eagle can't turn his head to defend himself. What the eagle does when pestered by the crow is a lesson we all can learn. He flies higher and higher and higher —up to a height the crow can't attain. The crows fall away one by one, gasping for air. When we put ourselves on a higher plane emotionally, we can out-soar the pests.

Eagles soar alone or with their mate. But it's best if you stick with your friends. Ask an adult for help and if you are an adult, ask a person in authority for help. Make sure your children see you standing up for yourself. Most of the time when two or three step into the situation together, bullying will stop.

Teach your children to be a friend and help someone walk away from a bully. Teach them to take a stand and tell your friend how to soar where the bully can't go. Teach them to ask the kid that is being bullied to play with them, to get as many friends as possible to come when you need help with a bully. *Pray for the bully.* The Bible says it's like putting red-hot coals on his head and maybe God wants to help the bully get over the hurt that has made him/her so mean.

Be an eagle. You are not a crow. Believe God's words about who you are. Don't believe the bully's words. You are an amazing masterpiece, made in God's image. He knows you and made you just as you are for a reason. He has a plan for you to give you a future and a hope.

> *But those who hope in the Lord will renew their strength.*
> *They will soar on wings like eagles.* (Isaiah 40:31)

Life Lessons: Does another person kick, hit, pinch, punch, trip, or threaten you? Does someone tease you, call you names, leave you out, or spread rumors about you? If so, they may be a bully. You can stand up to bullies if you are soaring to a higher plane.

Graduation Gifts

High school graduation day travels with us across the valley and mountains of our life, encouraging us to continue the journey. By passing this milestone, we know, beyond a shadow of a doubt that we can do anything. After all, we passed algebra while dealing with "mean girls" and raging hormones.

Fifty years ago, the Tulia High Choir sang, "May the Good Lord Bless and Keep You." I walked through the hallowed halls, across the stage, accepted my diploma, and moved the tassel from the right side to the left. Today, I hold tangible memories in my hands of the wonderful events and friendships we shared in the golden years of the early '60s. These treasures are not stored in the boxes of memorabilia I pull out every five years and show my kids, the grandkids, their friends, the dog, or any other being I can find willing to listen to stories of "back in the day." These treasures are used often … some every day.

I pull a hair band out of the miniature cedar-chest given to the 1964 seniors by Ramsey Furniture Store on the square at the corner of Dip Street and Maxwell. I dress and grab the wooden clothes brush, gold-engraved with my name—given by Ed Harris Men's Store—and remove the debris of life from my skirt before I head out to conquer the world.

On my charm bracelet with hearts from my twelve BFFs (best friends forever), dangles an icon of proof that I too defeated the dragon named "Algebra." (Well, I had a 70 and 71 average both years.) This charm with a maroon oval and a T on a golden crest, was a gift from Flint Jewelry Store.

Tucked here and there, or gone but not forgotten, are numerous other items we received from the good merchants to reward us for our hard work.

Back in the day, no one took graduating from high school as a "given" as if it was part of the Bill of Rights. You earned it. The merchants' gifts too were not expected, but were greatly appreciated.

The other gifts—the most important ones—are not tangible, yet are visible to the world. These real gifts lie within the students who cross the stage from childhood to adult, from being taught to teaching, from being nurtured to nurturing. These treasures aren't forged from metal or carved from wood.

The values that make self-disciplined, giving, caring, prosperous citizens—who love God and care for their neighbors—are bought by time and selfless sharing of one soul to another. Every event, game, club, class, homework assignment when kind caring adults helped us, made us who we are. We are like big, neon signs, flashing, "I was raised in Tulia, Texas." or "Hometown USA." The values given over the twelve years of school-years whisper in our ear.

All of their work, combined with our choices (some good and some not), made us. Here lies our work ethic, our morals, our desire to give instead of take. We have the tools we need to choose to succeed or accept failure, to rise up and become the adult our teachers and parents expected us to be or to remain dependent and unproductive.

It's a gift of graduation, a time to be a fledgling and fly from the nest. It's a time that says, we've given you our knowledge. Now what can you do? Like all gifts, it can be accepted or thrown out with the trash. It can be packed in a box to remembered only, but not used. For most of the classes that I remember I have to say the gift of education, paid for by the citizens of our community, was well done. And the students, turned adults, have accepted the treasured gifts and soared. In difficult economic times, the task becomes a struggle, but the outcome is always worth it. Thank you for the gifts.

Life Lessons: Give a graduation gift of time. Even if you live in a huge metro area, you can make a difference in your neighborhood. Start when the students are in kindergarten and continue until they graduate--give them encouragement, yet also give them consistent discipline. Shower them with love and affection, paired with responsibility and consequences. Know the hours you lavished on the young through 4H, church, music, drama, and sports will bring a high return to God's kingdom.

Leaving

We all leave our hometown eventually. If not physically, we leave mentally. It's leaving childhood and diving into reality.

There were so many "miracles" that happened to us from childhood through graduation, miracles that would appeal to all who were around during the time we grew up. Not everyone drove down Dip Street or lived in Tulia, Texas. Not everyone knew Papa or Mr. Howell. I didn't tell other wonderful memories like the Hornets Nest across from the Junior High that nobody was supposed to go to (I never knew why), the fire escape in the Junior High, Mr. Gatewood and how he ruled with an iron hand, Mr. Cook and what a sweetheart he was, or all the other wonderful things that made up the '50s and '60s. To survive the '70s we had to leave the '60s. But we placed the Happy Days in our memory box and pulled it out from time to time. Leaving childhood and headed toward the '70s.

Life Lessons: Encourage your children to leave you. Start in the church nursery when they are small. Continue until they are grown, leaving a little more each day, but always let them see you left the door open and the light on.

The Miracle of...

Driving Down Dip With Your Kids

Wedding Laughter

It was a beautiful wedding. The dresses, the candles, the flowers, especially the flowers, were wonderful. I worked at the florist for two years before the wedding; so my friends at work went a little crazy planning the flowers. The night of the wedding the candle glow and the smell of roses heightened the intensity of the ceremony.

"And do you, Peggy, take this man," the pastor was saying.

Yes of course I do. He's sweet and gorgeous and … I thought.

"I do," I said.

"And do you, Dickey, take this woman, Peggy…"

Yes, of course he does.

"Please kneel. Father, we ask Your special blessing on this husband and this wife," the pastor continued.

Wait, someone is giggling. I tried to look around.

"Bless their union," the pastor's voice was softer, as if he was distracted by the giggles. He was. I was!

Who is giggling? It's his mother! Why is she giggling? What does she know that I don't?

The pastor continued, "And, Lord, all of us gathered here promise to offer support…"

Not his mother, she's laughing out loud. And now everyone is laughing. Wait! I need to ask a question?

"May I introduce Mr. and Mrs...." The pastor continued although he still seemed a little confused at the laughter.

They're still laughing. The music swell filled the sanctuary and covered some of the laughter and this man, the one I'm no longer sure of, whisked me out of the church.

Wow!" I said with a catch in my throat. "They all seemed to enjoy the service."

Dickey had a funny look on his face and leaned against the wall. He lifted one shoe and then the other. "My little sister!" he groaned. Then he showed me the bottom of his shoes, and written there in big red letters the words—"Help ... Me!"

Life Lessons: Check your shoes soles before the wedding.

"Wedding Laughter" first appeared as "What's So Funny" in *Chicken Soup for the Bride* and *Chicken Soup for the Soul: Our 101 Best Loved Happy Ever After Stories.*

Parenting – Hell or Heaven?

Being a parent is a "life-changer!" It's finding yourself in the scariest place ever, knowing you are responsible for another's life and well-being. This small creature in your arms will succeed or fail in life because of your actions or lack of action. Everything you do is life and death for them. It takes every ounce of courage you can muster to be a parent. It's the most difficult, the most time-consuming and most exhausting role in life. It takes every penny you will ever have—all resources. It requires every brain cell and it never ends.

Being a parent is also the most wonderful, self-fulfilling part of life. There's nothing that compares. It doesn't matter if you are a parent by birth or by adoption. The greatest joy, the deepest love, the most prized accomplishment, is all wrapped in the bundle in your arms. The best part—nothing can ever take this being out of your heart, not even death.

Stephanie, our oldest, learned early and fast. She was a self-taught cook with 5 a.m. questions like, "Mom, what do you do when the fire is here, (has hand at eye level) "going to here?" (Her hand pushes as high as it can go.)

She prayed early, "Dear, God," she said in her sweetest four-year-old voice, rolling her big blues toward heaven, "Tell someone in there to get me some candy!" Or the time, about a year later, after an argument when she prayed, "Dear, God, please strike my mommy dead." Wow, I was in her school counselor's office first thing Monday morning, asking for help.

Once, when Stephanie was about eight, I heard her on the porch talking to the little girl next door. "Well," Stephanie said as she flipped through the pages of her Bible with all the pictures of Jesus in it. "I know it's in here somewhere and it says ..." From totally crushed to so proud I could float, this extremely smart child kept us engaged on the journey.

Cynthia, too, learned to pray early. She would come in with a problem and ask me to find a Bible verse. (usually verses relating to passing a test) Then she would say, "Write that down in your book, so I know it will happen." The next minute she would be in the backyard bragging to her sister. "I can use the "f" word if I want to, because mom can't hear me." Her big brown eyes popped when I answered through the open window, "Really?"

When Cynthia was a teenager, she mooned us during a deep-water dive in Hawaii. I laughed so hard, I almost drowned. My heart stopped once when Cynthia, at 25-years-old, pointed to a spot near downtown Dallas and said, "Jennifer and I spent the night there one night." I looked and asked, "There? That's a gas station." She laughed, "I know. But it had a light and we couldn't go to Jen's house because we told her mom we were at my house. And we told you we were at her house."

The most difficult moment for a parent comes when the phone rings in the middle of the night, "This is Presbyterian Hospital in..." The best time is in the delivery room and you see her holding her child and you think, *"Now she will finally understand how much I love her."*

The most challenging time—I watched my mom bury five of her children. How does a parent survive that much pain? The answer is a deep belief in the life hereafter. I know her love for her kids and their love for her remains—a bridge between heaven and earth.

A person who has never seen their child, still holds a place in their heart that can't be ignored. Being a parent, or surrogate parent, makes life worthwhile. The name might be

Mom, Dad, Aunt, Grandpa, or even Nana, but it rolls around in your memory and spreads sunshine on dark days.

Life Lessons: Forgiveness is a two-way street and there is nothing that cannot be forgiven. No matter what, tell your children that God loves them and you love them. Then show them—every day, all day long.

Giving Yourself a Birthday Party

When I turned thirty-three, I hated my birthday. I found myself in an emotional waiting room, dressed in my party clothes,wondering who would give me a party? Who would bring presents, bake a cake, blow-up balloons? Who would say I'm of value even though I'm getting older?

"Well, what do you want to do?" my husband asked in an exasperated voice.

"I ... I want ... I don't know," I stuttered, "something special."

"You want to go to the new restaurant?"

"No."

"Go out with friends?"

"No."

"What?"

"Something special, so I don't just feel old."

"Hmmmm." He disappeared into the garage. (I've always thought garages were built just so men had a place to escape.)

With no party in sight, I decided to give my own. How to celebrate? I couldn't really think of any event that would turn my depression into joy. I had no idea what I truly wanted or needed.

Down through the years, Christmas time had remained my favorite celebration. I loved to give gifts, especially to those who meant a great deal to me. This is where the idea to select a Birthday Person formed.

Now each year I select someone who has blessed my life. I chose my mom first. I was her eighth child. She gave me life and added a great deal of fun and love to my life along the way. Next was my sister, Ouida. We shared everything. Best of all, she shared her faith in Christ with me and many others. She died a few years after I made her my Birthday Person. We never know how long we have to say "thank you."

In the months before my birthday, I think of all the people who have blessed me. I search for a small token—a gift. Then I plan what I want to say. After writing my first rough draft, I get a clean sheet of paper that doesn't have tear stains on it. And then I create the finished product and mail it with a simple present. There have been many tears involved in writing notes to my Birthday Person, tears of joy, tears of healing—tears shared on the giving and the receiving end.

I've chosen a Birthday Person each year, all my sisters, brothers, daughters, youth directors, pastors, grandchildren, family, and friends—all have changed my life in amazing ways. Some years it has been more difficult to choose a birthday person and several times I've included a group—my Sunday School class, Facebook friends and more. It has blessed me beyond any gift I could have received. By focusing on others, I have eliminated the fear of more wrinkles and gray hair looming in my future. I'm amazed when glancing back over the copies of these letters to see many people on my list have now passed away—my mom, sisters, brothers, and friends. People who changed my life and who gave me so much, people I could never thank enough, now gone. I'm glad I thanked them when I did.

Thankfulness feeds a healthy soul within us. My "Birthday Person" celebration has spread to many of my friends. The healing power of saying "thank you" and praising others can keep you young—that and a box of hair color and really good facial serum.

I now look forward to my birthday. I hope you look forward to yours. Try celebrating with a thank you gift.

Life Lessons: In Psalms100:4 it says: *"Enter his gates with thanksgiving and his courts with praise."* In the culture of that time, the gate was like the courtyard or the entryway of a home, but the court was the living area—the place to be at home with special friends. Taking the time to say thank you and offering a little praise not only makes you happy, it can change someone's life, especially your children. Teaching your kids to say thank you and to praise is a huge gift to them. But the greatest gift is to teach them to be thankful to God and to praise him. Enjoy your birthday.

Matt

"What am I doing in a place like this?" I had turned down this job assignment two years before, but now it was this job, as an aide in the school for the severe and profoundly disabled, or no job. This was the oldest building in the district. The walls reeked with fifty years of sweat, vomit and vermin odor. It had been one of the city's most beautiful facilities; now it warehoused the students the administrators wanted out of sight and out of mind.

The small bathroom smelled of urine and human waste. The hard tile floor cut into my knees. I slung the jeans I had just pulled off the thin, braced legs of Matt, my nine-year-old charge, and grumbled aloud.

"I wanted to write songs and stories for you, God."

I had spent most of my three weeks at this job with Matt, trying to get him to go to the bathroom on the potty, put a block in a can or at least make eye contact.

To get him to look me in the eyes proved to be the most difficult. His eyes seemed to be the only thing he was able to control. He had no verbal skills, little motor control. All he had was the ability to look away or squeeze his eyes shut, anything but eye contact.

As I took the soiled underwear off Matt to clean his legs and bottom, I dropped the feces-covered underwear on my dress. "Oh, Matt, look what you've done!" I screamed.

He gave his soundless laugh and smiled, a grin made toothless from the many falls his wobbly legs had taken. Most days that smile would have melted my heart, but not today. My love was stretched thin, and my patience broke. "God, I hate this."

The small room grew still, and I felt Matt's stare. I glanced up and met his eyes. Large and luminous, they looked into mine, staring into my soul. In the quietness of the moment, I heard words with my heart—not Matt's voice and not mine.

"I didn't ask you to rewrite Sunday school literature. I didn't ask you to write songs. I said if you do it unto the least of these, you've done it unto me." Then Matt looked away.

God spoke to my heart in a most profound way in that smelly bathroom. In the years that followed, I learned to listen, and Matt taught me so many things. You don't have to be capable of seesawing to sit on one and enjoy white clouds in a blue sky.

Soundless laughter and silent tears often communicate better than words. Life in its most simple form is sometimes life at its best. Probably the best lesson I learned: God talks the loudest through the weakest.

Life Lessons: Teach your children to look for the good in disappointment, even when the plans are not those we would choose. Then take them with you to do for others—especially the least of these. Help them learn to listen and to search for God in all situations and in all people. As you teach your children, stay teachable.

"The King will reply, 'Truly I tell you, whatever you did for one of the least of these brothers and sisters of mine, you did for me.'" (Matthew 25:40)

Originally published in *Chicken Soup for the Soul: Devotionals*, Nov. 2011. "Lessons from Matt"

Jackrabbits

Today if you tweet, text or post a Facebook message telling the world of your weekend--how you shot rabbits from the back of your pick-up truck--you would be in trouble with several animal activist groups, the county sheriff and maybe the ATF. However, in the 1950s that was one of the things my family did often. We stood in the back of the old truck and daddy would drive and shoot at the same time. My brother stood in the back and shot over the cab. My sisters and I (without guns ... we were girls and not allowed to hunt.) stood around him. Mom had a spotlight and directed it from side to side.

I am now, and will always be, a believer in angels just because none of us died or were maimed for life. We didn't have on seatbelts. We didn't sit down in the back and we had loaded guns. Add to that the fact my dad never drove slow, not even bouncing across plowed fields and pastureland. Today, women's rights groups and Child Protective Services would also be calling. And if my grandchildren were in the back of the truck, I would be calling.

This was not just a fun event for Saturday night. We had to get rid of the rabbits before they ate our crops ... our beans, carrots, corn, tomatoes, greens, turnips, peas ... all the things we ate in the winter. If we didn't raise it and can it in the summer, we didn't eat in the winter.

In the book of Swisher County history, *Windmilling, the history of Swisher County Texas 1876 - 1977,* an account of the Big Jackrabbit Hunt was told by Will Jennings, except the story of the hunt took place in Castro County, probably due to the fact no one in Swisher County wanted to admit to the truth of the tale.

I loved the story of the Big Jackrabbit Hunt and I found it so captivating that I spent more than a chapter in my book, *The Coldest Day in Texas*, a historical fiction book set in Swisher County, retelling the story. (Although the Big Jackrabbit Hunt was said to have taken place in 1925, in my book I had it set in 1899. Writing fiction has its privileges.) The story works in a book for today's children because in it there were no guns and no dead rabbits.

"The rabbits were eating up the country," Will Jennings said. "They claimed there were 60 rabbits on every section." Swisher County had 900 square sections. Jennings continues, "That's a lot of rabbits. We got together here and had instructions on what to do. We were to go to the east line of Castro County, and line up to cover 30 miles around each of the four sides of Castro County for a total of 120 miles ... I guess there were 10,000 people. Some came from Lubbock and all around."

"The central location for the jackrabbit-drive included pens set up in Dimmitt, basically a prairie at that time. Everyone was to herd the rabbits to the pens that the organizers had set up. And there was to be dinner served for those in the hunt."

"We got over there at 9 o'clock," Jennings said. "... Fifteen miles to drive rabbits to Dimmitt. People about 20 feet apart. You could drive them a mile, but at the second mile, they would turn around and run between your legs. They'd run over you to come back where they were hatched and raised. We drove them two or three miles and gave up."

They were smart to have packed a lunch. Soon everyone gave up the gunless hunt.

I laugh each time I hear this story. Will Jennings tells it so much better than I do in my novel. His last words on the page are my favorite.

"You know how many rabbits I saw come into Dimmit? Three. I think they had a stroke. They were so weak they couldn't run back. Greatest joke ever. Ten thousand people learned a lesson that day they never forgot."

Life Lessons: It's hard to find a life lesson here or perhaps there are so many. "Laugh at yourself" comes to my mind. I would have planned this event if I had been around in 1925. Another lesson is to have fun with your family, using all the safety advice you know. Which may lead me to the best life tip. We can't judge what a past generation did—not killing rabbits, or no seat belts or riding in the back of a truck. They lived and made the best decisions they could with the knowledge they possessed. In the future, people may judge us for the decisions we are making and allowing others to make for us.

If something happens tomorrow and we have no power, no groceries, no way to provide for our family, what will we do? Will we worry about the little rabbits and allow our children to starve? Will we have guns to hunt for food and to protect our family? Will we live under tyranny where certain classes of society get food and the others die?

Life Celebrated

Where does time go? Somewhere in the universe, there must be one of those huge strips that catches flies and mosquitoes. However, instead of catching the troublesome insects, this colossal strip sucks time from our hourglass and swirls it down onto its sticky panels. I know, because just yesterday I drove down Dip Street as a teenager planning my future and now I drive down Dip Street remembering the past 50 years.

Back then, I wept as we buried old people. Today, I cried and rejoiced as we celebrated the life of one of my peers, a friend of my youth. And suddenly, we *are* the old people.

I cried for the world's loss of Harry Burton Lewis, missionary, teacher, good friend, wonderful preacher, servant, and prankster. But the tears were different from many funerals, because these tears celebrated the one who got to go to heaven first.

A large group of Harry's friends gathered for a memorial time of remembering, laughing and grieving together. Jim Smith, who left Tulia in 1962 to become a pastor and now serves as District Superintendent in the United Methodist Church, shared Harry's many accomplishments and younger days. Then Gay Roper Doan (a Christian counselor in Dallas) and Cynthia Robinson Hulett (a missionary and teacher) added comments from family and friends.

It was apparent that Harry's life, like the Apostle Paul, glowed with the fire of the Holy Spirit—passionate for Christ and engulfed with love for others. I remembered seeing Harry change in the blink of an eye at the altar of the Tulia

First Methodist Church. I remembered watching as the happy-go-lucky, fun-loving teenager become a "new person" full of light and love. The same thing had happened to me that year of miracles. I thought about the many worlds Harry had touched in and outside of Tulia—places like Japan. I felt honored to know him. Then I wondered, "Where did the time go and what did I do with those years?"

I loved celebrating Harry's life in a casual setting around dinner tables because it flowed from the heart of friends—real life, real love and really funny stories. As classmates and friends rose to tell of their memories, revealing Harry, the prankster, I learned more about Harry the person. I had only been involved in one of his adventures—the day we skipped school to go see the evangelist off at the airport. (Hey, we were Christian kids, full of the joy of the Lord and the usual teenage rebellion.) I was also involved in the six weeks of detention when we got caught. Other accomplices were my sister, a boy whose father was superintendent of the school system and Harry's little sister, who grew up to become the warmhearted editor of the Swisher County News.

During this memorial service, as one person after another talked about their friendship with Harry, we learned about mysterious missing-flags from the high school stage, table-knives placed in hymnals that clattered to the floor during college chapel time. And the most amazing discovery ... the case of the infamous headline ... "Beat Dimmit." Except the first "i" had mysteriously morphed into an "a" which took the rivalry between the two towns up a notch.

As the time of remembering our friend developed into tears and more laughter, I looked around the room. So many faces reflecting the love of Christ. Two precious ladies in particular, Mary Edwards and Emily Morris, laughed along with the rest of us at the confessions of pranks, skipping school and more.

Just then Emily Morris said, "I'm not sure I should have come to this. I thought you all were the best kids ever. I never dreamed you had done such things." She laughed and we all joined her. The comment reminded me of how blessed we had been to have adults like these two supporting the young people. They didn't go to Japan or Africa. They didn't become the heads of church. The two beautiful souls, like so many in Swisher County, served in a mission called Tulia, Texas. And I was one young person whose life changed because of them.

Life Lessons: All those who prepared meals, taught, gave, and shared Jesus every day--they grew our souls. Because of the dedication of the farmer volunteering as youth director and the businessman teaching Bible study, our lives were changed. People like Harry found life and left the little town to help change the world. God never wastes talent. He uses all of us in unique ways—if we are willing.

White Sands

When you face an impossible task, remember the sand dunes.

Each New Year we face disappointments of the past year and resolve to move mountains in the coming year. I used to have a New Year's resolution. However, no longer do I make resolutions. I break them too quickly.

I do love to set goals—goals with steps. The older I get, the steps are fewer and less steep. I usually have a goal for my spiritual life, my family life and my career. Sometimes the problems facing us are unknown. Other times problems hang over our head as the old year's midnight chimes. Then problems often travel with us into the New Year like an icy-cold, wet blanket.

For the last 20 years problems continued to find my husband and I. In times like these, when I'm faced by a mountain-sized problem, I remember White Sands National Park and the miracles I learned there.

Dickey and I took our RV to New Mexico and pulled a small trailer carrying his motorcycle behind. I had never been to that portion of the state and looked forward to seeing the White Sands. As we drove through the park on his motorcycle, beauty appeared around every dune. The sky rose high and the sunsets flared fiery pink and orange across the blue.

As we studied the printed information about the sands, I realized the miracle here was more than the beautiful cacti, animals and big sky.

In the White Sands National Park, winds whisper across the desert floor, "Move, mountain!" And the mountain of sand moves. In fact, the dunes of the Great White Sands move up to thirty feet each year. These enormous dunes roll and move like waves on the ocean, not with the help of bulldozers or giant diggers, but by one grain of sand at a time. The wind rolls these grains of sand. Sand is too heavy to fly through the air like dirt. So the wind can't blow it around, but it can lift it enough to move the mountain, one grain of sand at a time.

Sometimes in life, we face a problem that seems like a mountain. It's too big for us to solve. We fret and worry, trying to fix the problem, or sometimes we give up and go away. The problem defeats us and we feel weak and useless.

The good news is, God is bigger than any problem!

Life Lessons: Listen. When we face the mountain-sized problem we need to stop and listen. Hear the wind? Look at the problem? There is always one small, tiny piece of the problem that we may be able to change—one grain of sand at a time.

The Miracle of...

The Coldest Day In Texas

February 12th–a time to celebrate the record-setting temperature of 23 degrees below zero. The average minimum temperature in Swisher County is 24° F in January, and the average maximum is 93° in July. The coldest temperature ever recorded in Texas, -23° F, occurred in Tulia on February 12, 1899.

I can't imagine what the 150 or so families living in Swisher County during that time had to endure. Many times a blue norther would blow across the plains and shiver me to the bone. Once, it so cold I didn't think anything could live and those times the temperature was never much below zero.

The winters of 1956 and 1957 seemed to me the coldest temperatures I remember. A blizzard raged for three or four days. Dad couldn't get out of the house or even see the barn for three days. When the storm stopped, he had to go through a window to go feed the cows. The barn, covered completely with a blanket of snow, had a small hole showing. The cows' breath had melted that small hole. Our house was over one hundred years old and when the wind blew from the north our cabinet doors blew open. There was actually melted snow in our cabinet. We didn't have school for several weeks.

I can't imagine how the cold must have felt in 1899. The dugouts and frame buildings must have been icy. Those who settled our community survived hardships of many kinds. However, the coldest day in Texas must have been the most difficult. Without trees to block the wind or burn for heat, it must have been bitter. No microwave to heat your coffee! How did they wash the diapers and keep food on the table? How did they overcome depression and loneliness? The cold was bitter.

So why do we celebrate? We celebrate the people that survived it. I personally want to add another celebration. I celebrate those who are surviving the years of economic decline today. Their spirit amazes me. To keep on going, to love the land and one another, to encourage and help neighbors in the toughest times--they are heroes.

When you hold a record ... even a cold one ... you should celebrate it in a grand way. Host a Coldest Day Help Your Neighbor event. The small towns in Texas are the very best places on this earth--a great place to grow up and raise a family. The people are loving and kind. My hometown holds the record for the coldest temperature and I think the warmest hearts.

Life Lessons: Read *The Coldest Day in Texas,* a historical fiction based on that lowest temperature in Texas. Share it with your children and grandchildren. Order a copy for your friends. Oh my! This is a shameful advertisement. Yes, I did write it. Yes, you can order it on Amazon or Barnes and Noble or on my website: PeggyPurserFreeman.com

Prayer Meetings

My mom married at sixteen. Thinking back, it seems to me that she raised two families. I don't remember my oldest sister, Ladell, or two older brothers living at home. In high school, I didn't know my parents had ever attended church. My mom never spoke of church although she revered God; however, I never knew she had a personal relationship with Jesus.

I was in my thirties, when my sister, Ladell, the model and beauty queen, told me about Mom's miracles. The only word I can find to describe it is: Mom lived a life of "knowing." She always seemed to just know things. I think the Bible calls it a gift of knowledge. "I was about four or five," Ladell said. "We lived on the Oklahoma and Texas border. Mom took me with her to a morning prayer meeting. Suddenly, she stopped the meeting and said, 'We have to pray for the children." The others asked her why. She answered. "I saw the children tumbling through the air. We have to pray for the children." The group added a special prayer for the children. After the meeting, a man drove up shouting that the schoolhouse boiler blew up. Not one child was hurt, but the schoolhouse suffered a lot of damage."

I asked Ladell how someone with that much faith could stop believing. The answer I had to piece together over the years. Evidently my father was so involved in church he even led the singing. Then hard times became desperate times. Daddy lost his job and took work at his uncle's liquor store. The church they attended was very judgmental and asked my dad to resign his leadership in the church. My dad let this come between him and God. He started going out on the weekends--dancing and drinking. My mom knew she had to go with him or the marriage would break apart. She had been taught that she couldn't go dancing and to church.

Many years later, when my father died, my mom said, "I want his funeral service in the Methodist Church because my girls (Peggy and Ouida) attended the Methodist Church in Tulia and I KNOW they are real Christians."

Wow! That touched my heart! Later mom and I buried Ouida, Ladell, Naomi, Nolan, and Junior. I was so blessed to have that time to see mom's great spirit, to know the power of her prayers. I watched her grow in the knowledge of who God is, not the stern rule maker whacking the wicked, but a good Father who wants to love and be loved by his children.

I often wonder how life would have turned out if mom had stayed close to God. I wonder what kind of father my dad would have been if he had not taken the job at the liquor store, if he had trusted God. Or what if he had taken the job and joined another church, ignoring those who made such harsh judgments. The best choice always involves staying close to God—no matter the choice. *"If a hypocrite is standing between you and God, he is closer to God than you are."* Zig Ziglar

Life Lessons: Hard times require our best. The choices we make can affect generations. Go to church with your children. Don't let anyone stand in your way, not even your own pride. I know I will see mom in heaven. I will also see my dad there. But that's another miracle.

A Leap of Faith

At nineteen, my daughter dreamed of a modeling career. One Sunday afternoon she talked me into trying out as an extra on a movie being made in Dallas. We waited in line for hours. I had nothing but a business card, while my daughter presented her modeling headshot and contact card. We interviewed and they took a Polaroid of me. A few days later I got a call.

"This is Heather from Paramount Pictures Casting. Peggy Freeman, please."

"This is Peggy."

"You have the look Paramount Pictures is looking for as an extra in the movie *Leap of Faith*."

Oh, wow! I'm thinking. *The look Paramount Pictures wants!*

So I listened as she told me where to go at the studio, what to do and what to wear.

"Thanks." I said. "Now, do you want to talk to my daughter?"

"Oh, no." Heather cuts me off. "We don't want her."

"But," I stammered. "I only did this for her. She'll be crushed. I can't do it if she doesn't get to come too."

"Okay!" Heather groaned. "But tell her to try to look really ... dowdy."

"Dowdy? Okay. Thank you." I hung up.

Dowdy? Webster defines the word as "shabby, lacking taste, old-fashion." Hmmm! *Dowdy! The reason Paramount Pictures wanted me? Ouch!* I'm still trying to get over that one.

So we were in the movie. They paid us $75 a day and we did have a lot of fun.

My daughter and I performed as extras in the last scene of the movie. It was shot in the Paramount Studio in Dallas, the tent scene after the character played by Lucas Haas received healing and the townspeople rushed to the tent to praise the Lord.

Our part was to run in out of the rain, sing and worship. From 7 a.m. to 7 p.m. they sprayed us with water and we acted as if we were praising the Lord. For many of us it wasn't acting.

Recently I watched the show again, especially the end where you could almost see my wet arm waving. The point of the show remains profound. When the pure-in heart step out in faith, miracles happen. Like the boy in the movie who was injured by a drunk driver, we often discover that bad things can happen to good people. Sadly, there are those who hurt others for their own profit or pleasure. The miracle comes when we can leap beyond the circumstances of life and hold on to faith. We can believe the unseen until it is.

Like my daughter and I, many in Texas were in this movie. Like my daughter and I, you probably didn't become stars and move to Hollywood. Others of you may not have had the "look" Paramount wanted. But I hope all of you who saw the mean in this movie: a small community in desperate need of rain and prosperity can experience miracles when the pure-in-heart step out in faith. When this happens, you can get ready for the rain. If you step outside you can smell it before it comes.

Believe the light will overcome the darkness. Here in this country, miracles happen every day. Watch for them and believe. The blessings *will* rain down. We just have to take the leap of faith.

Life Lessons: Let your children see you solve problems, grieve, make mistakes and negotiate the family budget. Talk about the miracles that happen every day. Be sure when you talk about worries or troubles that you tell of the past when you overcame the hard times.

G.I. Joe

Born at the end of World War II and sheltered from other conflicts by a pre-tech world, Baby Boomers didn't understand the horrors of war until the 1970s. This generation immortalized war in movies and TV. It was no surprise in 1964 when the Hasbro Toy Company came out with G.I. Joe.

The history of this doll ... I mean "action figure" (I apologize to all the boys out there for that mistake.) is one that's based on a miracle.

When the Hasbro Toy Company needed a doll for boys, they looked for a hero and found Mitchell Paige. Retired Colonel Mitchell Paige thought they were kidding when they called and asked if they could use his likeness on a little Marine figure they called, "G.I. Joe."

Why Mitchell Paige? It goes back to one hill on the insignificant island of Guadalcanal and an unstoppable wave of Japanese with American soldiers' bodies stacked in layers. Only one Marine remained—Mitchell Paige. He moved all night up and down his line, pulling dead comrades off their guns and firing rounds of ammo toward the enemy. When dawn broke the next morning and reinforcements finally arrived, Paige was sitting behind a 30-caliber Browning. Paige received many awards, both as a member of the military and as a civilian, among them the Medal of Honor. And he had a G.I. Joe action figure designed in his likeness.

The next event in the life of the G.I. Joe figure was the year the company added a scar to its face. This came from comments made by consumers who felt the toy needed a touch of reality. One person quoted in the New York Times asked, "… why not have a G.I. Joe who bleeds when his body is punctured by shrapnel. Create one that screams when any one of his 21 movable parts is blown off?"

The company gave Joe a scar on his face. Somewhere between hero action figures and reality, our true heroes, those who are willing to give their life or limbs to buy our freedom, stand in the gap for us. They shield us from the horrors of war and let us remain untouched by its devastation. Many make jokes and skip over the rough memories, and others share how the bad times took them to a higher place—all keeping us safe in this sweet land of the free because they are brave.

Thank you to all who have served and are serving. We stand beside you to keep our country free from tyranny in all forms.

Hug freedom, don't let go.

Life Lessons: Honor those who have fought for freedom. Now it's yours to keep. You are the generation to pass on freedom. It may be your face on the next G.I. Joe.

The Miracle of...

Being a Parent

As I walked away from my daughter's first apartment, a tidal wave of emotions slowed my steps, engulfing me. This was supposed to be a happy occasion, toasted with congratulations and best wishes, that special moment in a parent's existence when they reached the end of parenting. I had looked forward to that moment when the credits would flash on the screen of life, when the chest fills with pride and a few tears of memory mingle with the joy of freedom. I longed for time to once more pursue the dreams I laid aside for parenting.

The past week of redecorating her bedroom into a study had kept my mind occupied. Seeing what was beneath the layers of dirty clothes that carpeted Stephanie's floor and discovering obscure cultures that grew on the dirty dishes under her bed had provided a comic reprise from that approaching moment of separation.

I turned to securely fix in my mind the memory of my little girl turning into a woman. The sun cast long shadows on the doorway, highlighting her blond hair. She appeared a perfect paradox, outgoing in appearance, but shy and timid in reality. Her blue eyes revealed a window into her emotions. She was a rosebud opening to the thorns of the real world. The weight of choices slumped her young shoulders as she said goodbye to childhood and stared into the future.

As she closed the door, the thud of the lock resounded in my heart. She walked to the bare window like she knew where she was going. Past experience told me she would not know for long. For the first time in her life, I could not control the way she would go.

I started the engine and drove away. A parent does not die from letting go, at least not in their adult child's driveway. "You can die at the corner or later at home," I whispered, "but, first you make space." I had tried to prepare to push my young fledgling from the nest, to college or to the army. Like the father of the prodigal, I had even considered the possibility of her running to a "far country" to "squander" her proverbial inheritance "in riotous living." I thought college would last longer than three days. The army was not an option. She would never consider joining an organization where the combat boots were not color coordinated with stylish fashions. That left me facing "riotous living."

Driving down streets colored purple with evening shadows, I listed the inheritance I wanted to bequeath to my daughter: peace, faith, and the self-esteem that comes from knowing you are a child of God. All these things I had planted and nurtured in her since birth.

Before she was born, I saw her as the perfect child. At two, I accepted the fact she wasn't perfect, but I was certain I could recreate her into a perfect adult because I would be the perfect parent—loving consistent, and all-knowing. By her thirteenth birthday, it was obvious I was far from a perfect parent, and I was no longer sure she would live to be an adult.

Now, leaving her in her first apartment, I felt old and tired, longing to know when it would end. When does parenting end? When would I stop worrying? Then I knew. *There is no end to being a parent!* Through my tears I saw the lights of the city. It crouched like a ferocious beast, waiting to devour my first-born child. "If there is no end to being a parent, how do I survive?"

The answer seemed to filter in through the vents with the cool evening air and settle on my weary soul. "**Let go.**"

I inhaled the night air, allowing its healing properties to sift through me. Glancing in the rearview mirror, I pondered my mother's dreams and unanswered prayers for me, all those things she thought I should do or be. She never tried to force them on me. She only watched "from afar." Watching from afar meant to trust my daughter with my most precious possession--herself. I admitted she would never learn to walk if I continued to carry her, never learn to pick herself up unless she was allowed to stumble, to fall. She would never see herself in the image of her Creator if I continued to stand in her way.

The city blurred past my windshield, dwindled into suburbia, then slipped into the darkness of the country. My daughter was changing and I had to change, too.

The pain of letting go gave birth to knowledge; God does not have grandchildren, just children.

Life Lessons: Move out of God's line of vision, so when your children fall down they will look up and see Him, not you.

The Miracle of...

Planting Seeds

Some seeds are so small it's difficult to see them, but they grow beautiful flowers, vegetables, trees. Some grow faith, hope and love.

Maybe it's the same in all communities. The church building may be different, the music varied, but for each of us we have memories of the place and time where seeds of faith were planted. Mine started at an altar in Tulia. Then other seeds were planted on the hillside of Ceta Canyon. One was at a Baptist camp at Falls Creek, Oklahoma.

My husband often talks of the white-framed, Methodist Church in Kress. His memories of sitting in the pews beside his grandparents, D.C. and Mary Beaty, warm his days with joyful memories of holding his grandfather's hand. In the white-steepled church, with his grandmother feeding him crackers to keep him quiet, the first seeds of faith were planted in him. He often tells me of the picture of Christ that still hangs there behind the altar, next to the choir.

"Even at a young age, I noticed the beautiful picture. The artist captured Christ's eyes in a manner that makes you know that he loves you." I heard Dickey tell many people about the eyes. At his cousin's (Deedee Beaty) memorial service, we saw it again. There were so many people at that funeral, people who knew Deedee as a child, as a teenager and when she returned to become one of the best teachers Kress ever had.

We were lucky enough to get a copy of the book titled *100 Years Kress United Methodist Church*. In this book we found a page written by Deedee. Here are her thoughts on that church and that picture:

"I'll never forget the night that I first dedicated my life to God. It was during a revival. For some reason, we were on the front row. At the end of the service everyone was singing 'Just as I Am.' I had my head bowed and eyes closed. Tears were running down my face as I felt a very firm hand on my chin. Opening my eyes to see who was lifting my face, I stared directly into the eyes of Jesus in the portrait behind the pulpit. The three of us [Deedee and two girlfriends] moved to the front almost as if we were one. We gave our lives to the Lord that night. I've never looked at the picture of Jesus since without remembering the feel of that hand on my chin, lifting my face up to see who my Lord is. When I walk into the sanctuary for any reason, my eyes automatically go to His eyes and I praise Him for loving me."

Dickey and Johnny Barnhart were great friends growing up. One day, as he and Johnny reminisced about the farm and the church, Dickey mentioned the picture. Johnny too remembers the eyes in that picture. The steeple bell held a special place in Johnny's memory, too. Here's Johnny's memory as it is recorded in the same book, *100 Years Kress United Methodist Church:*

"We lived on a farm five miles northeast of Kress. One beautiful morning, Daddy led me to a spot outside our home to listen to something that was not usually heard from that far out. It was the bell at the Methodist Church. That was one of the very first things that I remember and stays in my mind as a beautiful memory."

Life Lessons: Sometimes we forget to take the time to plant seeds. Other times we forget to nurture those seeds with hope, but the love those memories stir is still there. The faith a grandmother or a grandfather plants in our heart grows faith. A father, like John Barnhart, takes the time to teach his children to listen for something special, like church bells. He nurtures faith each time he lives that faith out in his life. Love grows from those seeds. The fruit that grows from those seeds is not only the love for family, but the love *for* God and the love *of* God. Share your memories with your kids and plant seeds in their lives.

The Miracle of…

Texas Independence:
Because of Travis, Crockett and Howell

I love Texas history—heroes like Crockett, Travis and Houston—all because of that other hero, Elvin Howell. That name didn't appear in the Texas history books. However he was a Texas hero, a teacher.

Elvin Howell taught me and a lot of other kids to love history. He pulled the characters out of our textbook and brought them to life on the second story of Tulia Jr. High School. Mr. Howell was a good basketball coach, always a gentleman, a great teacher and a lifetime friend. He taught us pride in country and state. Then he taught us pride in community and self. Each year as I celebrate Texas Independence Day (which I do with gusto) I also celebrate Mr. Howell and all the teachers who share their love of history.

I can just imagine Davy Crockett taking his stand on the wall of the Alamo as Santa Anna's massive army attacked. I still can hear Travis' "Victory or Death" letter he sent from the Alamo in my head as read by Mr. Howell.

The Republic of Texas lasted nine years, eleven months, and seventeen days, but the spirit of Texas lives on. Independence has always been important to the people of Texas. No matter what culture, no matter what shade of beige their skin, Texans choose independence and freedom.

Antonio López de Santa Anna became a dictator in Mexico in 1835. His brutality and his drive to take freedom from the Texian Anglos and Tejanos alike, produced a great outcry for independence. On March 2, 1836, a delegation met at

Washington-on-the-Brazos and adopted a Declaration of Independence. The Republic of Texas was born. When the Texas Declaration was signed, many settlers knew Santa Anna's brutality would follow. They headed eastward in what became known as the Runaway Scrape.

Those who stayed, and many who came to help Texas fight for independence, stepped into history as heroes. David Crockett, James Bowie, William Barret Travis, Stephen F. Austin, and Sam Houston stood up and fought for freedom and independence. On March 6, 1836, the brave men who fought for freedom at the Alamo fell to Santa Anna's army. On March 27, 1836, over 300 unarmed Texian prisoners were massacred at Goliad. Sam Houston's revolutionary army retreated eastward.

On April 21, 1836, at San Jacinto, the Texas army attacked Santa Anna's army while it was sleeping. In only 18 minutes, they defeated the Mexican army and captured Santa Anna.

Many, many heroes who fought for Texas Independence have not received the recognition due them. Like Brigido Guerrero, a soldier in the Mexican Army, who deserted to join the Texians when war broke out. Damacio Jiménez, a friend of Travis who brought in the eighteen pounder cannon, died in battle. Juan A. Badillo served in Seguin's Cavalry and was killed in battle. I could go on and on, but many Texian-Mexicans have not been honored as the heroes they were.

The stories of Texas' battle for freedom spread throughout the United States as Texas became a stable country, and in 1845 the United States Congress and Texas voters approved the annexation of Texas. On December 29, 1845, President James Polk signed the Joint Resolution of Annexation, admitting Texas as the 28th state.

Today, Texans remain fiercely independent and ready to fight for the nation, the state and the cause of freedom all over the world and at the ballot box. We need to celebrate as many events as possible in life, especially freedom. Freedom is one of the most precious commodities we have.

Remember the Alamo! Remember those who have fought in so many wars that give us freedom. Happy Birthday, Texas.

Life Lessons: Teach your kids history. Don't leave it only to their teachers. Take them to museums. One night a month, have a history night. Watch a movie that is based on history or read a historical or historical fiction book. By the way, *The Coldest Day in Texas* is a good one. (I know; it's a shameful plug.)

The Miracle of...

Fishing

I learned about life at the end of a fishing pole. To catch a sunset, a mess of fish and a cup of wisdom from my mom was a miracle, a miracle that shaped my life in so many ways. We went fishing as much as possible. My mom knew nature, such as where to catch fish and which bird sang in what kind of tree.

My husband's grandfather, D.C. Beaty, was one of the best people I've ever known and tied with my mom as the best fisherman. Once he said, "Tulia is the fishing capital of Texas. You can find great fishing within 400 miles any direction you go." He was right. At that time you had to go 400 miles just to find a real fishing lake. Tulia Lake did, from time to time, have water in it and sometimes a few fish.

My mom was born in the hills of Arkansas and raised on the river where her stepfather fished for a living. There were times of the year when she even had to go to school by boat. So living in the "Fishing Capital of Texas" was more than difficult for Mom. A few times she would take us to fish in Tule Creek, where it winds its way by Kaffir Switch. Yes, there was water there once...long ago. Our family vacation usually involved water.

Shortly after Dickey and I married, Mom and Dad moved from Tulia and bought a motel on a lake. Then my dad became a Realtor on Lake Livingston. Here my mom truly felt at home. She taught me and my seven brothers and sisters, most of her 25 grandchildren, many of her 34 great-grandchildren and wanted to teach her six great-great-grandchildren to fish before she died at age 94.

A few years before mom died, she and I watched through the large windows of her house on the lake as the sun painted the water various shades of orange. I loved the peace there. Suddenly a loud thump drew our attention from the sunset to the window that framed it.

"What was that?" I asked.

"Another bird," she answered calmly. She pushed up from her favorite chair and made her way out to the porch. Then she picked up a small cup of rainwater off the porch rail and stooped down to the small, still bird lying near the window. "They can't see the glass windows and are always knocking themselves out."

"Is it dead?" I knelt beside her. "What are you doing?"

"It may not be dead, just stunned." She tilted the bird's neck back and dropped a small amount of water on its beak. "I rub their neck, give them some water and then say a prayer for them. And they usually wake up and after awhile fly away."

My mom, what a sweetie, I smiled tenderly. "But the bird doesn't look like it's going to wake up. What will you do next?" Mom looked at me as if I should know.

"Oh, then I'll just chop it up and put it on my trot-line." She did and caught a few fish, thanks to that bird.

Mom was quite a lady. She held nature, animals and the world with the highest regard, but she was also realistic and left nothing to waste. I miss her.

Life Lessons: Take your kids fishing. God created nature for his pleasure and for ours. We need to teach our kids and grandkids to respect a quiet sunset and to enjoy catching a fish. Include how to clean and cook them in your training. Teach them to honor nature and protect it for the future without making man a prisoner to it. Get out into nature with your family. I believe fishing can teach a child to read, write and even do math better than any book. However, take a book along in case it rains.

THE MIRACLE OF...

History and the Great Indian Scare

In my novel *The Coldest Day in Texas*, set in Swisher County, I took stories from *Windmilling, the history of Swisher County Texas 1876 - 1977. Coldest Day in Texas* wrapped these historical events around the lives of a fictitious character named Shyanne Jones, her folks and siblings.

Written by heroes, *Windmilling* shares letters and stories of those who created a wonderful hometown where the rest of us could grow. The heroes? Poppy Hulsey, Gladys Goss, Mildred Loftin, Marge Hefley, Lucy Culwell, Gladys Ballenger, Kirk Hulsey, Helen Harman, Jack Keim, Jenelle Jordan, William Archie Jordan, Virginia Devin, Maxine Keim, Ellen Drake, Joye Braly, Dorothy Jennings, and many more—all heroes. Historians saving history. Writers saving stories of the heart. Teachers saving us from ignorance and pain. Heroes!

As you flip through the pages of *Windmilling*, you hear the excitement of new dreams and the heartbreak of old ones. I wish this book had been in paperback so more people could afford it. But with 618 pages, few people would read it instead of a vampire story. There's nothing wrong with vampire stories. It's just that all you've learned after reading one ... is don't fall in love with a vampire. You'll never agree on what to fix for dinner.

From history and historical fiction you learn about life and how to overcome. A perfect example is the "Great Indian Scare of 1890." This story is retold on page 34 of *Windmilling*, related by G.C. Hutchison who was fourteen at that time. (Source: Tulia Herald, July 11, 1940.) He tells how a drunken stagecoach driver roared into town spreading the alarm that Indians rode toward Tulia, on the warpath, butchering settlers and destroying homes.

As folks repeated the story, it grew like a prairie fire. Riders were dispatched to settlers' homes, to spread the warning. "Rush to Tulia! Bring your families and your guns." People dug trenches around the courthouse and the White Hotel. Posts hauled from the canyons were used for fortifications. At night, guards were stationed some distance from town. They would hold their ear to the ground, listening for hoofbeats or the redskins' blood-curdling war whoops. Ready, they waited.

They waited and waited, for two nights and a day. The excitement soon died down. Someone traced the tale of alarm and bloodshed back to the drunken stagecoach driver. He never came back to town. I might add that drunken tales of woe did return, probably more often than any of us want to admit.

Gossip burns and destroys far worse than any Indian scare. Having studied the life story of the First Americans, I dare say they had more to fear than the settlers in most cases. There were probably more poor souls killed by racing through the night and stumbling into a prairie dog hole.

I know more lives were destroyed by sanctimonious lips than by arrows. People so quick to share news, true or not, harmful or not—they raced. Once gossip was on horseback and at quilting parties, then on the party line and now through social media, tongues of flames destroying all in its path. Something inside us all wants to be the first to tell, the one who knows.

In the story of the Great Indian Scare, perhaps "the one who knew" was truly the fella with his ear to the ground. Words mean different things to different people, different generations. Don't listen to words. Listen for the sound of truth.

Life Lessons: When the men at the coffee shop share what happened on Saturday night, put your ear to the ground. When everyone around you acts like junior high mean girls, ripping another into shreds, put your ear to the ground. When the leader of the Women's Society to Save the World from the Wretched Sinners barbecues the local beauty operator, take off your hat and gloves and put your ear to the ground. Let your children see and hear you learn from history. Wait for the truth to catch up to the tale.

Home Sweet Home

Early in our marriage I found a verse in the Bible while studying how to pray using scripture. I read it in a modern version—a prayer about redecorating my heart/my home. It was the same week I joined a new study group that took turns hosting the meetings in the members' homes. The night before we had traveled to an upscale neighborhood not far from my small, but nice, home. I had been envious of their beautiful home and worried about inviting everyone to my place.

Suddenly, my hideous avocado-green carpet seemed to peel up from the floor and choke me. I hated it! I had it in the last house, had it in this house for seven years, and I hated it. If I died that night and reached the pearly gates only to discover avocado-green carpet, I would turn and leave.

When I found the verse about how God wants to redecorate "our heart … our house … our home," I prayed the verse over my yucky green flooring and wrote it down in my prayer journal.

The next night storms blew into town. Tornado-warning sirens roared. My husband flew in the door on a strong gust of wind.

"Get the girls and let's head to the underground parking!" Minutes later we huddled in the secure area at the mall with our neighbors. watching the storm roar. Hail pelted the city like softballs flying into centerfield. Cars sped into the underground parking area, looking like waffle irons on wheels. Hail damaged everything unprotected. Radios blared with reports of tornado sightings and rumors moved from car to car telling of rooftops flying across town.

When the storms died down and the calm of night settled, we headed home. The damage was great. One house gone, one untouched; neighborhoods without roofs; a block mowed down to nothing. As we turned on to our road we all let out a sigh of relief. Our house stood intact, only a few limbs and trees split. We unlocked the door and headed into the house. The gushing sound of water running greeted us.

"What's that?" my husband asked.

I worried that we might have left the water faucet on. We all searched for the sound.

"It's here, dad," our daughter called from her bedroom, where there was no running water, or at least there hadn't been prior to the storm. Rain poured from the ceiling.

"Well," I said. "I've been praying for God to redecorate my house, my heart's home. However, I hadn't planned it this way."

"I hope the insurance company was listening," my husband said as he surveyed the softball-sized holes in our roof.

We covered the damaged area in plastic as much as we could in the dark. Then we cuddled up for the night in the parts of the house untouched by the storm. We thanked God for the fact no one died. But the next few weeks brought me doubts. Maybe God was punishing me for asking for such trivial things like carpet. All the trial and trauma of cleanup from a storm covered the city. Neighbors helped others. Churches opened their doors, giving and sharing. It's amazing to watch the beauty of the human spirit in times of trial.

Slowly everything returned to normal. New houses even sprang up where the tornadoes ripped them from their foundations. The insurance company covered the cost of our new roof, minus its age. Sheetrock repairs and wood replacement was covered. My husband did the roof and the sheetrock. We learned to build and paint things and had enough money to replace the horrid green carpet.

Several months later I opened my door to my friends from the study group. The new carpet bathed the house in soft beige shades and the room glowed with the light streaming in from my new window treatment. Does God give us the desires of our heart? Yes! Is it easy? Not always. We'll never do another roof. But we did it, and somehow it all came together to work for our good.

Life Lessons: God does redecorate our home, but more than that, he redecorates our hearts—sometimes in ways we never dreamed.

Valentine's Day

Cupids, bears, hearts, flowers, and, of course, eagles symbolize Valentine's Day. Yes, I said eagles. I believe the eagle is the ultimate Valentine symbol.

Eagles mate for life. They are extremely committed. Courtship begins when the female flies in a circle and the male chases her. She notices his strong beak and takes note of his beautiful feathers, but the real test comes in his ability to face the storms of life, to manage when fate produces its sharpest decline and soars easily to a higher altitude.

The female gets a small leaf and flies to 10,000 feet or so and drops it. He dives at about 200 miles an hour, catches it and takes it back to her. She ignores him. Then she repeats the procedure with a twig and then a bigger branch. The bigger the branch, the faster he has to dive. Then she goes to about 500 feet. If he catches this one, she knows he can catch her babies when they fall. She can trust him. She goes on in the courtship. If not, she continues her search for the male with the right attributes to share life in the wild.

Eagles have been known to lock talons and drop toward the earth. Male and female pairs have also been observed with talons locked. The male will not let go. Even if it costs his life, he will not let her go until she releases. He's there until death do they part.

He brings her gifts, green twigs. As they nest, he has been seen stroking her feathers. He also brings toys to the nest—he says for the kids—cans, tires and balls of all shapes and sizes. Yes, the male species has many traits that are universal.

A few years ago I gave my nieces some Bachelor Button seeds to plant and told them the old wives' tale about how the little round flower helps you find a husband. But, it didn't take seeds to help the girls find a husband. Like my sisters, they are beautiful. And I bet their husbands could catch any branch before it crashes to the ground. Maybe the secret of the Bachelor Button seeds is that you have to wait a while to find the one just right for you.

I hope you know you are loved this February. There's a song, written and performed by the Gaithers, from a few decades ago that expresses why I've been married for 48 years... "I am loved. I can risk loving you, for the One who knows me best loves me more." I firmly believe that we can truly love when we know God loves us ... know from having experienced His grace. Because Dickey Freeman and I know how much God loves us, we have stayed together through many differences. It's that—and the fact I told him the first year we were married that "I do not believe in divorce, but I believe in murder."

Life Lessons: Tell your kids you love them and especially tell their mother/father you love them. When husbands and wives express their love for each other and show children that they love each other, their family grows in happiness and spirit.

The Miracle of...

The Stamp Store Thanksgiving

In 1964 two important things happened. Mom finally got real dining room furniture for our house on Crosby Street. And she finally used the savings stamps. Ouida, my sister, and mom's sister were coming from Dallas to Tulia to our house for Thanksgiving. I had licked thousands of stamps that Mom had been saving for years. These weren't "Green Stamps." They were "Gold Bond" and she had saved them to get a set of dishes. We had a couple of grocery bags full of stamp books. Early in November we drove into Amarillo to the store.

We bought china and glasses that matched, the first my Mom ever had. The dishes we picked out were a harvest pattern with brown and rich plum red and green apples on a bed of brown leaves on white china. The set was made in England. Then she picked out water and tea glasses in a colonial pattern stemware in amber glass. You can't imagine how proud she was of that table. Daddy had bought a dining room set for mom that year with a corner hutch that really made the dishes shine.

When I think back on all I've had, I love to remember that day mom went to the stamp store. It was bigger than Christmas—it was for her a lifelong dream. All the years of taking hand-me-downs left behind, cracked and chipped mismatched plates weren't much, but she had to work and pray just to have something for eight kids to eat, so dishes weren't important. Finally, with her last child about to fly out of the nest, she had a real set of china.

In 2005 my brother cleared out mom's house so we could rent it for enough to pay the taxes. Since Mom lived in the nursing home near me, he dispersed her meager belongs, hanging on to far more than he should have. He asked what I wanted. I had already talked mom out of several things, like the picture of Jesus holding the little lost lamb and the picture of Old Glory.

What did I want? One of mom's paintings and her book of prayers written out in a shaky handwriting that always slanted upward on the page. Prayers for her kids and grandkids, praise to a Savior she loved so well. I wanted those and the dishes. More than the white china with apples or the amber glasses ... I wanted the memory of the day mom and I went to the stamp store and my last Thanksgiving at home.

Life Lessons: This year when you sit down to Thanksgiving dinner, do two things. Let everyone say what they are thankful for. And then give thanks for your children. Say their names and tell God how grateful you are for something you love about them.

The Phone Call

In the spring of 1981 the girls of the Methodist Youth from Tulia spent the night in our home in Dallas. I was amazed at all the beautiful young faces that resembled their mothers and fathers, who had once attended the same Youth Group I attended. Twenty years before, I had gone on weekend retreats with them. The boys stayed in the home of another former Tulia alumni.

The next day my daughter Stephanie went with the group to Six Flags and came home bubbling about how neat they all were. The name Scott leaped into her conversation often.

A few days later the phone rang.

"She's next door. Can I give her a message?" I told the boy on the other end of the line.

"Tell her Scott called."

"Scott who?" I asked, because there were several Scotts, as well as Lances, Todds, etc. that called our house often.

"Scott Swinburn from Tulia."

I don't remember the rest of the conversation or hanging up. I was transported back to 1962. My sister, Ouida, and I drove up into a cotton field armed with Dr. Peppers and dressed to kill. Our prey, the Swinburn brothers, Dale and Max, had been our first loves and because of the Christian relationship we shared with them would always remain dear to us both.

"Scott Swinburn, Dale's boy."

Laughing, I reached for the phone to call Ouida. She would laugh too. She would...

Then I remembered ... she was gone. How could I have forgotten? What kind of sister forgets the death of the one who slept beside her for sixteen years and knew all of her secrets?

Having someone who shares your memories is truly a treasure. When that someone is gone, we understand the meaning of sorrow. I was so angry with myself. How could I have forgotten even for a moment? She had died several years before. As I thought, I realized when you share a memory with someone it is as if they are never gone. The memory spans the space of time and goes beyond the body. Yes, telephone lines are too short, but memories reach into eternity and touch those we love.

Life Lessons: Life is too short. Take care to always say good-bye and hang on to the memories.

Macaroni

I never knew my grandmothers, they both died before I was born. I did see my grandfather a couple of times and my great-grandmother once. Then in 1964 I suddenly had both a grandmother and a grandfather. I married the grandson of Mary and D.C. Beaty. I soon discovered "Ma" and "Dado" didn't really have grandchildren. They had kids. It didn't matter if you were their child, grandchild or granddaughter-in-law, you were one of "the kids." This was a miracle in itself, but the real miracle was, and is, Ma's macaroni and cheese.

I've never tasted food like her cooking anywhere else. It was just fried chicken, roast, turkey or (OMG) fried fish, but it was so much better. Her green beans, seasoned to perfection, often came from a can just like mine. Her mashed potatoes melted in your mouth.

We would come in from shopping (she was a pro at that, too) and Ma would say, "Let's fix tacos real quick." Mary and D.C. Beaty's decedents continue an ongoing competition to create recipes that taste "Just like Ma's." I've put everything I can think of into my macaroni, including egg like she did, but it's never exactly like hers. One of her real granddaughters, Jan Doan Meador, always tries to match the taste of Ma's cooking and comes as close as anyone. Jan whips up a batch of macaroni and then smiles and says, "Almost." It remains an unsolved mystery, a miracle.

Maybe it was the warm kitchen where you sat around the table after you stuffed your tummy full. Or maybe the laughing and talking for hours that made this such a special place. Maybe it was the soft sound of the washer and dryer every morning that gently lulled you into a peaceful state (washing clothes was one of her passions). Or maybe the love she poured into the cooking pot made her food the best. Even my dog knew. He would take his bowl in his mouth, sit up and beg for Ma's cooking. He never did that for me. Hmmmm?

Her sewing and designs were almost as great as her cooking. At one time I counted 350 little-girl dresses, with matching bonnets and little bloomers, in sizes six months to six years in my daughters' closet—all made by Ma. Each was a different style and different color, although many, many were various shades of blue.

Maybe the miracle included growing up in the 1950s and 1960s; maybe the soil grew a special flavor that seeps into families. Maybe because we made time for Sunday dinner. In those happy days, coaches never planned practice or games on Sunday. No one would have allowed it. That was family day. Dickey and I lived in Lubbock or Amarillo during our early marriage years. We knew we were always welcomed to their table. If you've ever tasted my cooking, you'll understand why we went home to Tulia for Sunday dinner so often. If you ever tasted Mary Beaty's food, you would have joined us.

Twenty-six years after she joined D.C. in heaven, we continue to try to discover the macaroni miracle. We continue to share memories of them, and most of all, miss them. The love of a grandparent is a lot like the love of God— it just is! Ma and Dado's love especially mirrors God's love. God doesn't have grandchildren either—just children.

Psalm 34:8 says, *"Taste and see that the LORD is good..."* especially at Ma's table.

Life Lessons: Strong families create strong children. Time is a major ingredient in creating strong families—time for dinner, time for church and time to simmer into productive, happy adults. Tell coaches no Sunday game or practice. Tell the church no committee meetings after church on Sunday.

Just as Sunday morning belongs to God, I believe Sunday dinner/afternoon belongs to the family. And remember, it's not the same in a restaurant. Give your children time with their grandparents. The grandparents will teach them many things and the kids may teach their grandparents things, like how to use the computer.

The Miracle of...

Singing Harmony

When the Blues, Country Gospel and the electric guitar had a collision in the '50s, harmony rocked. Even lyrics like, "Sh-boom, Sh-boom" and "Bom ba, hey nonny ding dong, alang alang... dip a dibby dobby dip... life could be a dream, sweetheart ..." It was a harmony explosion, but I couldn't sing harmony.

Singing and driving go together like Dr. Pepper and ice. Rock 'n' Roll has immortalized the drag. 1960-1965 produced more songs about driving, dragging and cars than any other time. "Mustang Sally," "409," "Little Deuce Coupe," "G.T.O." and "Fun Fun Fun" are just a few greats. Other generations added "Greased Lightning" and "When God-Fearing Women Get the Blues." Driving down Dip, singing at the top of our lungs, could delight and de-stress at the same time. But I couldn't sing harmony.

I sang high soprano in high school. Mrs. Sponholtz, the choir director, taught me music and taught me to believe in myself. I didn't have a gift for music, but I could fake it. She encouraged me to fake it. No matter how hard I tried, I could not sing harmony.

In the last ten years, I've been blessed to sing and play in a dulcimer group, the Brazos Country Strings. I am honest enough to tell you they didn't let me in the band because I'm gifted with playing the dulcimer. A dear friend gave me a mountain dulcimer about 20 years ago and I still struggle even though it only has three strings. I can't really read music. I'm with the group because the amazing and dear dulcimer man of Hood County, Howard Hayre, asked me to sing harmony with the group.

So, how did I learn to sing harmony? Mrs. Sponhotz taught me to sing and Howard Hayre taught me to play the dulcimer with authority, but you can't fake harmony, although I've heard people try. Harmony was a gift from my Uncle Franklin.

True, the gift of harmony wasn't wrapped up in pretty paper and tied with a big bow, but it was a gift. No way could I have earned it. It wasn't a "birth" gift. It was delivered when I was in my thirties, sometime in the fall.

Franklin A. Purser, was the best, truly a godly man. At family dinners, his wife, Bess, my Aunt Pearl, Aunt Texie and my precious Aunt Flora fed our bodies with everything from fried chicken to homemade ice cream. Then Uncle Franklin pulled out his old, well-worn accordion and fed our spirit with song. My dad would harmonize with him. As I grew older, Franklin harmonized with me.

The last time I saw my Uncle Franklin, we both knew it would be the last. At seventy-nine, losing a five year battle with lung cancer, he finally stopped going to the nursing homes to sing for the old and the sick. He lay in a hospital bed at his daughter's home, so I let myself in quietly.

"Hi, darling." Franklin's smile, though weak, lit up the room. I hugged him and we shared the unimportant topics on which people waste precious time. But I finally took a deep breath and told him how much he meant to me.

"... and, Uncle Franklin, can I ask you a question?"

"Yes," he answered and blinked his dark French eyes and smiled.

"If there's any way you can, when you go through those pearly gates, will you leave me your ability to sing harmony?"

He laughed softly. "I will if that's possible."

I kissed him and left him sleeping. He died a few days later.

About six months later, I heard it, somewhere between my brain, my ears and my vocal cords. It ebbed slowly, and then came like a parrot's call that fills in the sounds it usually hears. I began to perceive the thirds—two notes below or above the melody— and sometimes another note would fill the gap. Now, I oftentimes can't sing the melody if an instrument or others are singing it. It's as if Uncle Franklin's voice is there leading the way.

In our dulcimer group, it's the same. I will be humming and singing a song around the house and suddenly I hear Howard's voice sing a phrase, or Glenda Smith's high harmony, or Tom Petry's tenor. I can now harmonize as Debby Fishencord plays a strong melody on the mountain dulcimer. Tying it all together is Jim Sexton's guitar and then the others. Each in their own way adds to our group with their gift, a collage of sounds weaving the old, old stories and the toe-tapping tunes.

God's plan is a symphony of harmony. I learned this fact from lucky people like Terry Templeton, who have seen a slice of Heaven. He explains it as "nothing you've ever heard, not one song, but all songs, sung together and it creates a beauty no words can describe."

Life Lesson: If you want knowledge on anything, ask for it. God is the intellectual creator. Try asking for a gift you admire in others. Who knows; you might even be able to play golf better. I'm asking for my Aunt Flora's grace and regal stature. At 93, she is amazing.

Scratches on the Pews

I traveled into New York City by ferry over a year after 9/11. Ground Zero stood like a gaping wound, fresh and raw. I walked around it, read the graffiti on the wooden boards, noted the prayers and curses—sadness and hope.

At lunchtime I ate at a deli nearby. Two fireman sat at the table next to me and, with my usual Texas friendliness, I tried to start up a conversation. I truly wanted to express my thanks for all they had done. When I commented on how difficult it must have been for them, one quickly stood and walked away. The other cleared their empty baskets and nodded my way. "It's still very hard to talk about it. Plus, so many people come from out of town and don't understand." And I knew he was right. I had no idea the pain they suffered.

The church near ground zero, St. Paul's Chapel, an Episcopal church, had housed and fed recovery workers throughout the entire nine-month Ground Zero cleanup. It had sheltered those rescuers. The pews had been the bed for weary workers. The private pew, where heroes like George Washington had worshipped, was used by podiatrists to treat burned, blistered feet, replace boots and repair the shoes of the workers.

At the time I visited the church, it had been restored. New blue carpet replaced the soot stained runners, and the walls had been painted a fresh white coat. I sat in a pew to say a prayer for our nation, for protection, for healing. Then I noticed the pews were badly scratched.

Why didn't they repair the pews?

When I stood to leave, I saw a sign. It explained that the scratches on the pews were made by the tool-belts of the workmen who rested there. The workmen who had ministered to the hurting, searched for the dying, had rested there. Here they had refueled to go back out and continue to search for those to save. The church decided not to repair the benches. They believed all church pews should bear the scars of those who come there to rest.

In the years since the terrorist attack on our nation, we've all had to deal with the fear and worry. We've grown complacent at times, and regained our hope for peace at other times. We continue to believe in freedom, to fight an enemy of hate and to trust in one another. We are all called, now more than ever, to hold on to our freedom. We resolve to let no one scare us out of our freedom or buy us out of our freedom. And most importantly, I pray we remain "One nation under God..."

Life Lessons: When you're weary, find a church where you can rest, a church that allows the pews to be scratched and imperfect. Hold your children and remind them that good days always follow the bad. Show them that things scratched are not as important as the person who scratches them. Never cease to rescue the perishing.

The Miracle of...

Senior Citizens Dragging Dip Street

A Death Threat

When Dickey and I first married I told him, "I don't believe in divorce, but I believe in murder!" He laughed. I didn't. It worked. Our marriage has been perfect...perfectly wonderful...perfectly difficult. As we celebrate our 50th wedding anniversary, I echo what I told him in 1964.

"I don't believe in divorce, but I believe in murder!"

The Miracle of the Sequoia

Long ago, when dinosaur feet made deep ruts on the land, seeds fluttered into shallow soil and burrowed deep into rocky crevices. There the seeds rested in dark warmth, softened in the rain, then swelled, growing bigger and bigger until one day they popped open. Small green sprouts twisted out of the seeds, through the soil and reached toward the sun.

The sprouts grew into seedlings and the seedlings grew int large trees. Then needle-like leaves that pointed toward the heavens. Different from the other plants, these seedlings refused to lose their needles or turn brown in winter. These trees remained ever green, ever growing, ever reaching toward the sky. Short and fine, the roots of the giant trees grew close to the earth's surface, all of their energy poured into the quest of growing taller.

For millions of years, decay bit at their massive trunks. But these giants contain tannin to protect its bark from disease. The wood, tough and coarse-grained, fights off insects. The trees refused to grow bark close to the ground. When fires spread across the land it only slowed the giant tree's growth. Giant sheets of ice ripped the evergreen's shallow roots from the earth, until only a few remained. They clung tenaciously in the mountains and continued their quest for the sky.

Now, only a few giant trees remain in a small section of the forest by the Pacific Ocean. Tremendous rains wrestled the top-heavy trees and wind-gales blasted up from the shore, attacking the giant trees. More giants fell. Nature attacked at the weakest point—their shallow roots. Easily dislodged, one by one they toppled.

Here nature used an amazing spiritual truth. The shallow roots of the giant trees stretched toward each other. Short, fine roots wrapped around and around, then intertwined into a massive ball. The beginning of one root or the ending of another can't be found.

The winds continue in this part of California. But the giant trees, having gained strength by joining their roots, stand firm. They stretch toward the heavens reminding all who stand in the shadow of their massive trunks of the power in working together.

The giant evergreen was eventually named "Sequoia" the name given to the great Cherokee, Sequoia (Sequoyah). When he saw his people ripped from their homes and watched the gales of political injustice divide them, he gave the people roots, roots to reach out and hold on to one another.

Unable to read, write, or speak English, Sequoia created an alphabet, an alphabet to communicate like the white man. With that alphabet Sequoia gave the Cherokee their history, their heritage and a voice to stand up for their rights.

Like the Sequoia trees, the Cherokee Nation still stands as the largest of the Native American Tribes.

Life Lessons: Today our economy, our freedom and our values are under attack. I believe our roots will help us survive. Like Sequoia, we have to communicate in order to protect our history, our heritage and our rights. We must teach history to our children, pass down values and continue to guard the Republic our founding fathers gave us.

Hand in Hand

Images of my mother's hands fill my memory. At the sewing machine until all hours of the morning, making biscuits, planting seeds, my mother's hands worked from early, early morning to late night as she cared for my seven brothers and sisters and me.

Mom's hands bore the scars of many mishaps, like defending herself from my fishing hook, the small catfish I flung at her, or a sharp knife as she taught me and my sisters to make jelly. Once, while she rushed to finish sewing one of our dresses, she pierced her hand with the needle of the sewing machine. She carefully stopped the machine, pulled the needle out and doctored the bloody wound herself.

Mom's hands never stopped. In between the cooking, sewing, washing, ironing, and making us mind, she worked in the fields with my brothers and my dad. When the cold weather turned leaves on the cotton stalks brown, my mom would rub her sore hands, put on the worn work gloves and walk back into the fields to pull any cotton that might have been left. With this money she might have enough to buy us a pair of shoes or a toy.

I was twelve when my parents were able to lease a farm and mom didn't have to work in the fields. After twenty-eight years, she finally had time to paint. Like the lives she nurtured, the art her hands created wasn't always perfect but it reflected all her love.

When I became a mom, my daughters' hands also intrigued me. When they were babies, I loved to patty-cake on their hands. Later they held my hand to walk, then they let go and ran. I held their hands when they learned to pray, when they suffered with a fever and when they skated down the sidewalk.

Twice in my life as a mother, I have had the incredible joy of holding my daughters' hands as they suffered the pain, and experienced the amazing miracle, of childbirth. Their white knuckles gripped my hand and I hoped they knew the joy coming into their lives. As their babies grew, accidents and illnesses have brought our hands together again. My daughters come to me, fearful for their children, and I do what my mom did; I hold their hand and pray.

Of all the memories I have of mothers and daughters, the last days with my mom fill my heart with the most amazing love. At 94 mom's health had declined. I had held her hand as she cried for the loss of my dad and five of their children. These losses were the hardest for her to endure. I struggled through the trial of how to help her as she grew older. Finally, I held her hand as she entered a nursing home.

For four years I visited with her almost daily and enjoyed her even when she wasn't sure who I was. Then one day the nurse called me mid-afternoon.

"Hurry, I'm not sure how long she has," the nurse said.

When I got to the center, the nurse met me at the door and shook her head. "I'm afraid it may be too late."

I rushed to mom's room. There was no sound, no movement. "Mom," I said as I took her hand. A quick intake of breath made an audible noise and mom moved her fingers. Her eyes fluttered but remained shut. I wasn't too late. Or maybe she returned to hold my hand one more time.

I sang her favorite hymns and read her a description of heaven. Then I held her hand and sang "I'll Fly Away" as her soul flew to heaven where I have no doubt she holds the hand of her mom and grandmother, not to mention my sisters and brothers.

One of my greatest joys remains hands ... my first grandchild's hands touching my cheek, my granddaughter taking my hand to go on an adventure, my young lady granddaughter taking my hand for the first time and wrapping her fingers around my heart.

Life Lessons: The hands we hold transport our hearts into a life of love and service. From mothers and daughters to granddaughters and grandmothers—from fathers and sons to grandsons and grandfathers, we are blessed by amazing relationships. Our hands can heal or they can hurt. It's a choice. We can be the hands of love.

The Miracle of...

The Kidney Stone

A few years ago there was an urgent plea for an adult male to go on our church's Junior High Mission trip. Without a male volunteer, the youth wouldn't get to go. So my husband told the Youth Pastor that he would go.

My mouth dropped. "Dickey Freeman with junior high youth in South Texas in July? No way!" But he felt the Lord wanted him to go.

The week before the trip, Dickey's old friend, another kidney stone, attacked. He was in pain from Sunday afternoon to Thursday morning, barely able to walk much less pack and get his work done around the house. Then on Friday, he woke up without pain. Kidney stones usually move around on him for a better position to send a barrage of pain until he can finally pass them. I was so concerned, but prayed for his healing. But the kids from our church wouldn't be able to attend unless he went; so we packed his bags and he headed to Galveston. Their mission was to do much-needed repairs for some families in that area. The mission clients lived in Texas City. The group was divided and Dickey had a crew of new kids, six twelve and thirteen-year-old kids and two young-adult men, who didn't have any experience in construction. Their task was to build a new 12x14 foot deck with a ramp, tear down and put up new kitchen cabinets, remodel the bathroom, replace the flooring in both bath and kitchen, and replace the plumbing in the bathroom—all in four days.

This is how Dickey described the trip: "When we drove up to the site, I looked at the stack of supplies delivered to our site. The only thing that came to mind at seeing that mountain of work was the Country Western song, 'Jesus, Take the Wheel.'

"I thought we would share our faith and joy with the family, but our client was the one to raise our spirits with each smile. It was difficult working around all of her children, grandchildren and extended family that she had taken in to raise. I think there were twelve in all. At first the children shied away from us, but by the end of the week they were so mixed in, we just became one big family.

"We worked non-stop except to laugh and share our lunch and devotions with the family. We worked, sang, laughed, and played most of the night and then we would wake up early to do it again the next day. On the last day I wasn't sure we would make it. But my teenage crew pulled through, even the one boy that said, "I don't really like to work." A twelve-year-old-girl put together a huge porch swing all by herself. I screwed in the last screw as our time was up.

"The miracle wasn't that we finished an amazing task. It wasn't the fact these kids did amazing work. Nor was it the fact that an old man didn't collapse in the middle of the week. The miracle was the relationships that developed."

Sunday morning, back home in Granbury, Dickey and I sat in church, energized by the experience. The kids had the same glow on their faces. Having been on mission trips myself, I understood the awe they felt. Then in the middle of the sermon, Dickey grimaced. I knew the pain had hit again. He broke out in a sweat, and shortly after church, he passed a kidney stone about the size of a matchstick head. He said the pain wasn't too bad. I knew he was still on the mission high. Nothing could erase the joy of the week he had experienced.

Miracles come in all sizes and sometimes happen in the middle of a kidney stone attack.

Life Lessons: Don't doubt the feeling of doing something against the odds. If God has a plan, doors open and pain waits. Consider taking your kids on a mission trip. There are many groups you might join. Even the kids who don't like to work find the experience life-changing.

The Tale of the Two Tails

A farmer needed to plow his field before the spring rains came or his family would surely starve. However, he had no team to pull the plow. He searched and found a donkey and an elephant. Now the donkey, named Progressive, was always forward moving. The elephant, named Conservative, didn't always like change.

The farmer hitched the donkey and the elephant to the plow, yelled, "Haaa!" and the donkey took off at a breakneck speed, only to be brought to a sudden stop. The reins snapped the donkey's head backward and his eyes bulged. He turned, searching for the problem.

The elephant stood firm and loudly trumpeted his protest, "Just where are you going so fast?"

Now the farmer tried and tried to get the two to work as a team because his family would soon starve. Finally, the farmer unhitched the two.

Unleashed, the donkey took off at a breakneck speed, running faster and faster, until he ran off the cliff, crashed on the rocks below and was never heard from again.

The Elephant, untethered, looked around and then sat down and slowly sank into the miry mud pit, never to be heard from again.

The farmer felt abandoned and worried for his family. He decided to try again to plant a crop so his family wouldn't starve. Searching far and wide he found two extremely intelligent animals—one named Future and one named Past.

Now Future was also a forward-looking creature. However, he carefully considered each direction and the consequences of each action. Past wasn't keen on change, but after carefully considering how things had been and the outcomes that came with the actions, he would move forward.

The farmer hooked them to his plow and cautiously yelled, "Haaaa!"

Future saw the need to move quickly to save the farmer's family and started to take off like the wind. Then seeing cliff ahead, he stopped. Past saw Future move to fly forward and, remembering the donkey and the cliff, he sat down. As quickly as he sat, he remembered the elephant and the miry pit and stood. Then Future and Past looked at the farmer and listened and thought carefully as they plowed the ground with new seeds of hope for the farmer and his family.

Oh, that Future and Past would come today and plow the fields for the USA.

Life Lesson: When cruisin' through life, watch the road before you, but keep an eye on the rearview mirror.

A Sojourn

If you ever talk with many widows about the next life, you will eventually hear of the "visit." Once I enjoyed a Bible study with about six widows. One day the subject came up—a sojourn from their loved one on the other side. Three of the precious ladies told of seeing and talking to their husband. As they talked I remembered my mom told me about seeing my dad about six months after his death.

"He looked younger," mom had said. "Maybe thirty-five or so and he wasn't sick. He told me he was okay. And he had our little dog with him. He reached down and gave the dog a chicken breast. He told me to be happy."

After mom shared this, I had the courage to talk about my experience of communicating with my dad at the point of his death. I find sharing this story difficult. I don't want people to think I'm weird. Oops, too late on that one! If you know me, you already think that.

My father was having a brain scan to see if his lung cancer had progressed to his brain when he went into cardiac arrest and was placed on a breathing machine. The doctors documented it as clinically dead. A breathing machine pumped air into the chrysalis that had housed my dad's soul and then pulled it out again with heavy grotesque sounds. This would continue until the family asked for him to be removed from the machine.

During this time, the family stayed at a hotel near the hospital. On the second day, mom and I drove out to their

151

home on Lake Livingston to transfer money and make arrangements. I sat on the porch swing, trying to quiet a variety of emotions. Sadness and anger warred within me.

Daddy, I am so angry with you. You left things in a mess. There was no insurance, no money and mom has not worked for 45 years.

Suddenly I felt a chill. It was more of a stirring than a breeze. I knew instantly it was my father and he had been searching for us. I also knew he didn't like the fact that I judged him so harshly.

That night, back at the hotel, I went to bed knowing that I had to go to the doctors the next day and ask them to remove the machine. I lay quietly praying for the courage to do this. As I prayed, I once again felt the stirring. I prayed:

God, this is my dad. I want him to know I forgive him for all the things he did wrong, and please take him to heaven.

I saw my father's hand in another hand, a hand with scars and I—perceived more than heard—Jesus' voice:

"I know your father. He met me when he was a boy."

Just as quickly as I felt this experience, it disappeared. However, an amazing peace flowed through me and I knew my dad asked for my forgiveness for the wrongs done over the years, and he accepted my prayers for him.

All this can be explained away by a psychologist—the brain wanting closure. Just as those who don't believe contrive all kinds of crazy excuses for death and afterlife experience to avoid the truth. There is a heaven! We will see them again.

In the past few years, having lost my siblings and mom, I've wondered why I haven't had the chance to communicate with the others, especially my mom. How I would love to see her and tell her how much I love her. But we said that all before she sailed away over the Crystal Sea. She and I left nothing unsaid or undone. I am so thankful for that time with her and grateful for the miraculous opportunity to see my father's hand in the hand of Jesus.

Life Lessons: Be open about the miracles in your life. There may be someone in your life who needs to hear them. Share past miracles and expect future ones.

Birds

I love birds. Wild or tame, they delight me. Recently I sat on the patio enjoying a spring morning. Birds sang and a cool breeze whipped the smell of freshly mowed grass across Pecan Plantation's 6th golf tee. Several birds were fluttering around my water fountain when this wonderful little bird hopped up to see me. I think she was on her way shopping or perhaps to the bank and I was in her path. She hopped up on the glider where I sat and then skipped behind my back. I turned my head and she hopped down to the ground.

I thought she was gone, when suddenly she jumped up on my lap, tilted her head with a quizzical glance at me and then sweetly left a deposit on my leg. A few minutes later, she returned. I hoped she would get in my lap again but my dog scared her away.

After a little research, I knew it was a Tufted Titmouse. I wish you could see how beautiful this little gray bird is in person. Actually, you can. There are so many great bird-watching sites in our state beyond my backyard.

One of my favorite bird stories explains Easter in a way that even little ones can understand. The story goes that a farmer started his morning the same way each Sunday. His wife dressed, ate and begged him to join her for church. He mumbled regret about too much work and admitted that he didn't understand her belief and saw no reason to pretend he did. Why would anyone believe a story about a God coming to earth as a man to die on a cross?

One Sunday near Easter an unusually late cold front blew across the farm. The farmer woke early to check on the stock. He had a second cup of coffee and watched the snow fall. Then he noticed a few birds huddled under the eaves of the house. This small bird was a variety that didn't stay in the area all year. For some reason they hadn't headed south before this cold blast. The farmer knew the birds wouldn't make it through the night. He decided to open the barn doors for them to fly into its warmth. But the birds stayed huddled in the cold. Then he scattered breadcrumbs toward the barn. The birds still didn't move. He threw rocks and yelled, flapping his arms like a crazy man. The birds fluttered and then returned to what they thought was safety.

Frustrated, the farmer looked around and tried to think. "If only I could find a way to tell them to go to the barn," he said to himself. "If only I could become a bird for a moment in time and show them how to be saved."

Just then the church bells echoed across the snow-covered fields. Suddenly the farmer understood. His wife dressed warm to drive to the church as always, but today, the farmer joined her. Now he understood why God became a man. And yes, he left the barn door open.

Life Lessons: I hope you know that God became a man to show He loves us. Children often have trouble with concepts based in religion. One of the best ways to explain is by using relationships. That's what the Bible does. Too often churches put big-word labels to explain simple relationship terms. The farmer and the birds express part of this in a relationship we all understand. Take time to celebrate a relationship with God.

The Arms of God

And the sun came out... We opened our doors after the stormy night and stepped out into the sunshine.

The spring of 2013 brought devastating storms to Granbury, Texas, the town where we now live. Having been raised in the Panhandle, seeing funnel clouds whip across the sky between Happy and Tulia, I knew the clouds that day held destruction. Remembering Silverton's killer tornado of 1962 (Silverton the town near Tulia holds the record of 65 tornado events over a category two), I hurried to the nearest shelter or closet.   In 2007 another devastating storm even dared to assault Dip Street and ravage Tulia.

When we lived in Grand Prairie in the 1970s the city was impacted by such storms. Many homes were decimated. Ours was damaged.

None of this prepared me for the ride through Granbury's Rancho Brazos subdivision. I know ... knew this area well. Several years ago the Methodist Church we attend held Vacation Bible School on a vacant lot there. The church had a relationship with many of the homeowners because of its work with Habitat for Humanity.

Hood County Habitat for Humanity has built four or five homes each year since 1996. With over 100 Habitat homes in the county, most of them in Rancho Brazos, the community pride and "work to get it done" attitude developed into our church buying the vacant lot, building a structure, working with the Hood County Boys and Girls Club, setting up tutoring sessions, and building a ballfield, playground and more. The building offered a place for community meetings.

Like one boy said in his prayer one day, "Thank you, God, for a safe place to shoot pool."

After years of leading singing with those sweet children, teaching them Bible verses, watching them grow and getting to know their families, the sight of the destroyed homes and vacant slabs hit me in the gut. Those homes weren't built with money, they were built with sweat and love. Now, street after street, where our church bus once picked up smiling faces, looked like a bulldozer had plowed through, leaving mounds of rubble. Many, many foundations stood bare. All of the magnificent oak trees were snapped like pencils.

I relaxed a few hours in the closet on that stormy night, eating chili and reading a book, as my husband watched from the garage (Why do men do that? There is no way they can get to the closet fast enough if the cloud decides to drop down.) As Dickey watched the tornado pull up and slip past us, we had no idea those dear children and their families were losing everything they had—some their life. Later I felt like I had somehow cheated my neighbors just a few miles away.

Our home is within the arms of the Brazos in Pecan Plantation. Look on any map and you'll see the river loop around and almost touch itself, just south of the Lake Granbury dam. There bad storms, including tornadoes, roar up to the water's edge and the majority of the time the storm clouds split or turn and the funnel clouds rise. The clouds move on and then descend on the other side of the river, where, once again, the river often lifts the low-hanging clouds. The Brazos, or as the Spanish called it, Rio de los Brazos de Dios, basically means the Arms of God. I believe the river saved so many homes and lives in the storms of 2013. It wrapped around us and hugged us as the storms passed.

It's difficult to understand why storms destroy and kill. People say, "God protected us." Does that mean He didn't protect others? Or does it rain on the just and the unjust? I believe God loves us all and allows a testing at times. He also has a time to be born and a time to die for each of His children. It's His job to know and control those things. It's our job to do our best to look out for each other and to listen to the laws of nature. To take shelter and face the storm in the "shadow of His wing" because He is our help.

However, the river does hold a power to protect. It's not magic or a miracle. It's the power of the river. Canyons often have the same effect. Mountains can cause a cloud to move upward too.

One lady told of being in her bathtub in her home in Rancho Brazos Estates during that storm, feeling the winds lifting her and then, ever so gently, a pressure pushing her back down in the tub, almost like God's hand holding her there.

We are hugged by the arms of God, whether we are protected by the river, a canyon, the only hill in the county or by God Himself. For there is a time for every purpose under heaven. Whether we outlive all our friends or beat them to heaven, it's about *how* we live and love. That starts with knowing we are loved. *"For God so loved the world that He gave his only begotten Son, that whosoever believes in Him ... has eternal life."* [John 3:16]

Life Lessons: Teach your children how to be safe in the storms of life and tell them to not watch a tornado cloud from the garage or the street or the yard, but from the shelter of His arms.

Don't Stop ... Keep Going!

The first time I met Monte, he was complaining about everybody celebrating his 99th birthday. It was hurting his chances for a date.

"No woman wants to go out with a hundred-year-old man," he said with that infectious laugh I often heard over the next few years in the church lobby where he ushered three services each Sunday morning. Celebrating his birthday didn't do too much damage to Monte's social life because I saw him out with two different ladies that next week. I learned that Monte loved people and enjoyed getting to know them.

A 99th birthday isn't something celebrated every day and I decided to interview Monte for the magazine I edit. Some of my interest in Monte stemmed from a nagging thought that I might be getting old. I had recently found myself in a room thinking, "What did I come in here for?" And my day involved looking for ... glasses, keys, book, letter, address.... Well, you know. The interview with Monte was the first of three, the beginning of a friendship I will always value and a change in how I handle aging.

Monte was a chemist and advanced the efforts in World War II by keeping his Fort Worth plant open and running at high production during those years. He delivered Meals on Wheels until he turned one-hundred. At one point, they wouldn't let him deliver meals anymore because his driver's license had expired twenty years before. I think he was a better driver than I am.

When told he couldn't drive, he didn't sit inside and feel sorry for himself. Nor did he argue and drive anyway—breaking the law. He asked someone to drive him down to take the test. His neighbor volunteered, thinking it to be a waste of time. Monte passed the written test with a score of 100 and the driving test with flying colors. He received his new driver's license and continued helping the old people.

I asked him for his secret to long life. He did recommend lots of water, not overeating and to learn new things.

"The main thing is," Monte said, "I don't stop. If I wake up with a pain, I just put one foot in front of the other and I get going. I keep on doing."

Most of that doing was volunteering in the community, in the church, in the neighborhood. Monte was interested in others and stayed busy.

On my last visit to his house, he was raking the yard and answered my question regarding his health.

"Well, I'm feeling quite well," he said. "Except this one knee is giving me a little pain. I'm not sure what's wrong with it."

"Monte," I answered. "It could be that the knee is one hundred years old."

"Well, yes," he laughed. "And it's about to be 101."

This is when I evaluated Monte's zest for life and willingness to serve others. As an author and editor, I find myself sitting far too much. After Monte passed away, another friend came my way, one I could serve the way Monte had served others. My knees have been hurting a great deal lately, but "I just put one foot in front of the other and I get going. I keep on doing." ... and I keep on learning. If I hear of a new technology, I try to learn as much as possible about it or how to do it.

Helping others ... old people with knees that hurt ... keeps me young. I try to swim every day possible. I have learned to play an instrument and, with a group of friends, visit nursing homes every week. Helping others has helped me.

I believe in finding a quality that I admire in the people I love and applying it to my life. Then part of that person will live on through me. I believe Monte's motto ... keep going and keep learning ... has kept me from sitting myself into bad health and slow thinking. Now if I can find my keys, I'll be ready to go help others.

Life Lessons: Just put one foot in front of the other and get going.

The Miracle of...

Broken Bones and Buttonholes

My husband, Dickey, and I celebrated our 45th wedding anniversary looking forward to retirement and an active lifestyle.

We traveled the month of July across the southern states, visited family, joined our grandkids for a vacation, and searched South Carolina for ancestors. After enjoying a successful vacation, we drove back home to Texas.

Three days after our vacation, our active life came to a halt. Dickey crashed his motorcycle and was care-flighted to a major hospital thirty miles away. Everything on the left side of his body was broken except his toes and ear. Even his right shoulder suffered a fracture, a rotator cuff tear and nerve damage. He woke up angry with himself for having crashed his cycle. He had ridden 750,000 miles without an accident, not even a ticket. My thoughts consisted of how blessed we were that there were no head or internal injuries.

Three surgeries, three weeks and caring for fourteen broken bones later, he came home from the hospital and rehabilitation center to conquer life with a wheelchair, a walker and numerous other devices.

Exhaustion soon overcame my emotions of thankfulness. I thought life couldn't get harder—however, it could and it did.

On a beautiful day in September, I wheeled Dickey outside to look at the damaged cycle. A dripping water faucet drew my attention, and I scurried to turn it off. On my way back from the water faucet, through the flowerbed, my bad knee caused me to trip. As I fell, I managed to avoid hitting

Dickey's broken leg but I fractured my left elbow. The next week, the EMT first responder to Dickey's accident, dropped in to see how he was doing. James Green and his wife, Patricia, lived a few blocks over and were friends. After he left, I took our little Shih Tzu out in the backyard. The late afternoon breeze offered a little relief from the heat of the day. Suddenly, a dark shadow flew over the yard. A hawk swooped down toward our dog. I hurried her toward the house, but struggled with my left arm in a sling. Once again my knee gave out. I tripped on some rocks and slid toward a stone wall like it was home plate in the World Series. With my left arm in a sling, I lay there, looking at my right wrist, bent and definitely broken.

Not one golfer was on the course behind our house. Not a neighbor in sight and a husband in a wheelchair, I finally pulled up to a sitting position and located my cell phone where I had dropped it in the rocks. Using my left hand, I called everyone close by and then remembered what our friend, the EMT, had said only minutes earlier. "Call if you need anything."

Now, four broken arms and two injured legs between the two of us made the difficult next to impossible. Thanks to our daughter, neighbors and many great friends, we were well fed and our house was clean. However, there are some things neighbors can't do, like button your jeans. This is where "for better or worse" pays off.

"You push; I pull," I explained to Dickey as he pushed the button through the buttonhole. Then I waited to pull the button through to the other side. It may have taken us thirty minutes to button our jeans because we had to stop to laugh from time to time.

Then there was the day his Velcro got stuck to my Velcro. I needed help wrapping my weak knee with an Ace bandage. I stood in front of Dickey so he could toss the bandage over my knee while I handed it in under my knee. The Velcro on my bandage stuck on his super-duper Velcro on the boot protecting his broken ankle.

Sometimes you just have to sit down and laugh. Injuries and illnesses are two things that can't be avoided in a marriage. Recovery and rehab can be extremely difficult on a couple, but it can also give the opportunity to practice giving —giving even when it hurts to give. Literally hurts. Like opening a drink bottle with two broken arms so the one you love can have a Dr. Pepper. One of us would hold the bottle; the other would use a nutcracker to unscrew the bottle top.

It takes a great deal of humor to overcome times like these, or maybe times like these create a great deal of humor. It also takes tolerance. My husband bought a new motorcycle.

"Listen to that motor!" he crooned.

No, I'm not thrilled when I hear that motor! However, it's not really my decision.

The other side of marriage is giving space and acceptance. Life is an adventure. Knowing there is someone who will be there no matter what, giving to you as you give to them, is the true meaning of marriage.

Life Lessons: Creating a good marriage is the best way to love your children. Providing a safe place where children see people treating each other with kindness, surviving hard times and having a sense of humor gives your children skills to survive their own future—good and bad. Worshiping God together also gives a head-start on creating a happy marriage.

The Miracle of...

Dip Street – Always in the Rear-View Mirror

No matter where you go in life, you are never too far from the main drag. This became a fact in our lives just recently. My husband and I had worked non-stop on this collection of stories, all tumbling through our mind much like a tumbleweed in a dust storm. Sometimes quickly rolling along and other times, snagged by a memory—lingering long enough to say, "Remember when..." Our thoughts swirled with memories of old friends, Dip Street, and long ago. One weekend, we drove from Granbury down to Brownwood to help with a stone-setting service for William A. Fisk, a hero of Texas, a Texas Ranger and a General in the War Between the States. While we were there, I planned to gather information for some other magazine articles. One happened to be on the Lehnis Railroad Museum in Brownwood.

Due to construction, we circled three times to find a place to park. When we pulled into the parking lot, an old wooden train depot, sitting at the back of the block, caught my eye. I looked up and the word "Kress" in big brown letters on the yellow depot drew my attention.

"Why is Kress on that building?" I asked Dickey.

He studied a moment and said, "I don't know, but it sure looks like the one in Kress, Texas."

To our surprise and delight it was the very train depot that welcomed the many trains that rumbled and roared through our Panhandle towns. When automobiles became abundant and the train depot closed for good, the building was sold. A man who had been a welder on the railroad bought the old Kress depot and moved it to the Brownwood area.

We took pictures, asked questions and called old friends, telling them of one memory that had literally followed us to North Central Texas.

Life Lessons: We are never too far from home. Surprise and wonder wait around the curve ahead, and sometimes the present and the past collide to create a new memory for tomorrow.

The Miracle of...

Life

Too long. Too short.

So hard. So easy.

Complex, simple.

Exhausting, exhilarating.

So bitter, so sweet.

Sinful and ugly.

Redemptive and beautiful.

Sad. Joyful.

Too long. Too short.

Life

The Rose Garden

The Garden—

Words do not come easy when surrounded by quiet beauty.

Fragrance whispers too loud to hear fearful words screamed from the heart,

Dewdrops out-sparkle any tear.

Iron gates open to tranquility for those whose hearts weary of storms outside

Crashing against its stone walls.

The Bush—

Graced with beauty and thorns, the bush flourishes under the Garden's pruning.

And when its tender shoots face disease or the evil of pestilence,

It rests quietly, knowing its roots

Will support the bud, however that bud chooses to grow.

It fears not, but turns to the sun and holds tight to its belief.

The Bud—

The bud, so new and full of promise, smugly sits on top of the bush,

Ignorant of its own selfishness, it holds its perfume tightly within.

Soon it will fade.

Wilting, it will anguish over the regrets of its youth.

Unaware of its mortality, it can't comprehend the openness of the full bloom.

The Blossom—

The rose, open full face to the light, seems not to resent the new bud,

Nor fear the faded bloom, but simply to give of its beauty,

Not holding back, for autumn lingers near.

To all who dare to reach within the thorns,

The blossom gives freely the fragrance and enchants the heart.

The Petal—

Dried and pressed, the petal silently flutters to the ground.

There it appears useless and spent; quietly it begins again.

A faint essence laced with love remembered,

Strengthening those left behind.

Decaying, it promises life eternal—beauty everlasting—

love till the end of time.

It All Fits Together

This last entry was inspired by the last words my sister, Naomi Ruth, spoke. She's the sister who rescued me when I fell behind the big iron bed when I was only a few weeks old. Ruth was only seven years old. Unable to move the heavy bed, she crawled under it, scraping her back on the metal springs. She was my second mother and my best friend. In the last days of her life, as she drifted in and out of this world, she didn't talk for a day or so. Then suddenly, she sat up in the bed and said, "It's amazing how it all fits together."

It All Fits Together

It's amazing how it all fits together.

It's an incredible sight to see

When heaven and earth become one

We'll be amazed how it all fits together,

Arm and arm in the light of the Son.

The Last Word

The Lord God of Israel says: Write down for the record all that I have said to you.

Jeremiah 30:2 [the Living Bible]

About the Author

As the eighth child of a sharecropper, I know it's truly a miracle that I'm here in the first place, that I could possibly be an author and that you have chosen to read my work. For me the craft of writing is difficult, but I love stories and the sharing of stories.

I was born in Dallas, Texas, and have lived in most of the small towns that had work for a large family, including: Wills Point, Robertson, Idalou, Caprock, Ralls, Lorenzo, and some I may not remember. Tulia will always be home. Since Dickey and I have been married, 50 years now, we have lived in Dallas, Grand Prairie, Arlington, Alvarado, and Cedar Hill. Now we live south of Granbury, where the Brazos River hugs the land.

We have been blessed with many, many excellent friends. Although all of my brothers, sisters, mom, and dad have crossed over, I am so blessed to have approximately 75 nieces, nephews and greats and great-greats. My grandchildren and my daughters are amazing people. Dickey is such a good man and our dog is the best ever.

Peggy's works include:

The Coldest Day in Texas (TCU Press), one of three finalists for The Texas League of Writers Teddy Book Award, which was presented by First Lady Laura Bush. Set in 1899 Swisher County when the temperature reached a record setting low of 23 below zero. [Available on Amazon.com and through Barnes & Noble.]

Swept Back to a Texas Future – a historical play for children depicting an overview of Texas history. (Hendrick-Long) Music tape is available.

Cruisin' Through Life: Dip Street and Other Miracles celebrates the '50s and '60s, inspires family values and transports the reader back to home and heart in a Lewis Gizzard fashion.

Spy Cam One-the First Dog and White House Security(TanMcAli Publishing) [Available on Amazon.com]

Chicken Soup for the Soul Anthologies:

Devotional Stories for Tough Times
101 Best Happily Ever After
Think Positive for Great Health
Teens Talk to Middle School
Chicken Soup for the Bride's Soul

Other Anthologies:

Chips Off the Writers Bloc
Christmas Chips from Granbury Writers' Bloc

Coming in 2015:

In the Shadow of His Wings – Family Devotionals based on the eagle

The Cheer Squad: My Sister the Cheerleader, Vol 1
Something to Cheer About – Devotionals

Editor – Peggy served for the past 10 years as Editor for Granbury/Glen Rose Showcase Magazine.

Freelance Writer – Peggy writes for major magazines across Texas. She has written columns for newspapers and written and presented for Radio Disney 620AM public affairs shows.

Speaker – Peggy speaks on: her own work, the writing process, Texas history, responsible behavior, values and finding your own family history.

Teacher – Peggy has taught continuing education writing classes at University of Texas at Arlington and Texas A&M Tarleton's Langdon Center in Granbury.

Student Writing Workshops – Students of all ages love writing when they participate in Peggy's workshops. Centered on games and fun activities even writing becomes an enjoyable adventure.

Texas Independence Day Student History Fair – A 2014 Volunteer of the Year for the Texas Heroes Foundation, Peggy serves to promote Texas History and the freedom and liberty we enjoy as Texans as she facilitates the TID Student History fair in North Texas.

www.PeggyPurserFreeman.com

peggy@peggypurserfreeman.com

Made in the USA
Middletown, DE
07 July 2024

56757358R10097